The Ultimate Outdoorsman's
Workshop Handbook

The Ultimate Outdoorsman's
Workshop Handbook

A Fully Illustrated Guide on How to
Organize, Maintain, and Store
All Your Outdoor Gear

Monte Burch

The Lyons Press
Guilford, Connecticut

An imprint of the Globe Pequot Press

The Lyons Press is an imprint of The Globe Pequot Press.

10 9 8 7 6 5 4 3 2 1

Text designer: Sheryl P. Kober
Printed in China

ISBN-13: 978-1-59228-866-3
ISBN-10: 1-59228-866-9

Library of Congress Cataloging-in-Publication Data is available on file.

Contents

Foreword

Most outdoors people are do-it-yourself people. Part of that comes of the physical necessities of living the outdoors lifestyle, and the rest comes out of the desire to have things done the right way; in other words, done right *your way.*

With this book, *The Ultimate Outdoorsman's Workshop Handbook,* author Monte Burch shows you how to do it your way, the right way, every time. That might sound a bit odd—having someone else show you how to do things your way—but everything Monte teaches here is intended to become yours.

That's because the goal of this book is to help create a proper platform for your fishing and hunting adventures and improve the quality of those experiences through proper organization and preparation. Each of the book's seven chapters—Gun Storage, Gunsmithing Tools, and Projects; Fishing Tackle Storage; Hunting and Shooting Sports Equipment Storage; Stands and Blinds You Can Build; Boating, Camping, and ATV Storage and Equipment; Dressing, Butchering, Skinning, and Tanning; and Knives, Axes, and Other Sharp Tools—contains a primer on the necessary tools for that particular endeavor. Included, too, are a set of adaptable plans for developing stations and systems for maintenance, storage, and repair, and easy-to-follow instructions for essential projects.

Consider the chapter on Fishing Tackle Storage: after describing the proper tools the do-it-yourself angler must have, Monte goes on to tell how to set up a proper rod-and-reel repair shop, how to create a rod-building jig and workbench, how to make a rod-holder for wrapping guides, and more.

Need to work on your rifle? Check out the plans for building a rifle holder. Got a messy, insufficient reloading space? Read through the plans for creating a reloading bench and supplies cabinet.

Repairing your arrows? See the instructions for creating a fletching jig. Too many dull blades? See the chapter, Knives, Axes, and Other Sharp Tools. Too many decoys? Here are plans for sorting and storage. Can't keep track of all your hunting clothes? Ditto.

Possibly the most enjoyable contents of this book, however, are the designs for self-made gear: how to build fishing rods, make bucktail-jig heads, turn out and paint wooden plugs, make a recurve bow, and construct your own basic hunting knife. Creating and then using such implements successfully in the field would be a point of personal pride for years, and properly maintained, a number of these items could last a long time.

At what might be called his handyman's estate in rural Missouri, Monte has worked for nearly two decades as a full-time outdoors writer and gear tester, evaluating everything from bass boats to ATVs to chain saws. His numerous articles have appeared in *Field & Stream, Outdoor Life, ATV,* and others. Contending with the physical and technical demands of such work for so long has led Monte to some keen insights on the way an outdoorsman's workshop should function. For him, a proper workspace and storage are the necessities of his livelihood. For the regular outdoors person seeking the best way to keep gear operating at optimal levels, Monte's instruction is invaluable because you can't put a price on a great hunt or a great fishing trip, yet your success is ensured, in part, by how you handle upkeep at home.

So, as a professional and as an angler and hunter, Monte has lived the lessons contained in this book. When he and I worked together in the past as writer and editor, respectively, at *Field & Stream* magazine, he designed one of the most elegant yet simple and useful do-it-yourself duck-boats I had seen, a project that, to its credit, you can still find posted on the *F&S* website. Monte has explained to me any number of times over the telephone how "you just cut this like this, and that part goes there," and while I had no problem understanding his instructions, every time I've talked plans with Monte, I've realized he's a natural-born designer who thinks in 3-D and can construct anything piece by piece in his mind.

I once hunted feral hogs with Monte, and another time fished for salmon with him, and I realized that the man's breadth of knowledge extends way beyond the number of books he has published. A dedicated bow hunter, hard-core crappie fisherman, and pro in the seat of an ATV, Monte Burch could dispense valuable advice in bucketfuls, if he wanted to. But he is the most easygoing deer-camp gentleman you'll ever meet, and you'd never know, just talking with him, that he could do more with the average toolbox than the Army Corp of Engineers. But eventually you'll realize that you could drop him off in the middle of nowhere with a pallet of plywood, nails, hammer, and saw and then go back in two weeks, and he'll invite you up for a beer on the deck of his backwoods chalet and not speak a word about having to put up a roof by himself.

—Scott Bowen
Editor, The Lyons Press
November 2006

Introduction

It's easy to collect a lot of outdoor gear, regardless of your outdoor passion or pursuit. Hunters, anglers, campers, boaters, ATV and gun enthusiasts can all quickly end up with a garage full of stuff, and a frustrating, can't-find-anything situation. Organizing gear into specialized storage areas can not only get rid of the clutter, but protect your valuable investments. We show you how to build a variety of cabinets, racks, and other projects that can organize and secure your gear, even a shed for boats and ATVs.

A major factor is often repairing, maintaining, or even building or customizing outdoor equipment. Also shown and described are the tools needed for these chores, whether gunsmithing, rigging decoys, or working on your boat motor.

A number of special outdoorsman's workshop projects are also included, such as a stand-up sight-in bench, a sight-in shed, tree stands, and many others.

I am a longtime outdoor writer, as well as a gunsmithing, how-to, and wood-working writer. I am lucky enough to have a full shop of the latest, as well as many antique, tools. Many of the projects in this book, however, can be constructed with just a few hand tools. The projects range from the very simple to the more compli-cated that require more time, tools, and experience. But even if you're a beginner in do-it-yourself or woodworking skills, don't be intimidated. You can build projects to organize your gear and do basic repair and maintenance chores to your outdoor equipment with little or no experience.

—Monte Burch
October 2006

The Ultimate Outdoorsman's
Workshop Handbook

CHAPTER 1

Gun Storage, Gunsmithing Tools, and Projects

Working on guns is a very pleasurable hobby that can not only help maintain your investment, but also help add to your collection. Maintaining, cleaning, repairing and customizing guns can run from the very simple to extremely complicated, requiring special tools and skills. The amount and kinds of tools and storage you'll need depends on how involved you become in gunsmithing. Also the type of storage for guns and tools depends on the number and types of guns and how involved you get in working on them.

WORK SPACE

You'll need a space to work. Gun work doesn't require as much space as some of the other crafts, such as building large projects. A lot of gun work can be done on your kitchen table. A place set aside with a small, but sturdy workbench and storage for tools and supplies, however, is much more convenient. Two factors should be considered in finding a location for your gun work, humidity and security. One of the worst places you can set up shop is in a damp basement. In this type of environment, within a month or so most of your tools, guns and gun parts will become badly rusted. An unlocked building is also not a good choice. Not only are unsecured guns, tools and cleaning supplies dangerous to small children, they're an open invitation to thieves.

If you have a dry basement, it can work, or any other small room in the house that can be locked. Other choices include a separate gun-working room closed off and lockable in a garage or a securely locking outbuilding. The latter should also have barred or other securable windows.

Although guns look great stacked on racks along the wall, the best storage is a gun safe. An alternative is a metal or wooden cabinet that is bolted to the floor or wall and has a sturdy locking door. You will probably also need one for storing dangerous equipment or chemicals such as blueing compounds or other materials that should be kept out of reach of small children.

Workbench

One of the most important things in a gun shop is a good, sturdy workbench. The bench should be of a comfortable height so you can work at it standing up or seated on a tall stool. Most gun work will be done while standing. If you use a stool, one corner of the bench should be shaped so you can get your legs under it while seated on the stool. The bench top should be smooth, a rough top makes it hard to see and handle small gun parts. One solution is to cover a bench with a piece of $1/4"$ hardboard. If it becomes roughened with use, simply replace it. We have included plans for two workbenches, one fairly complicated and one simpler bench. Plans for both are in the Projects section of this chapter.

A secure place to work is important for working on guns. You'll need a sturdy bench, a good overhead light and a place to lock up tools and guns.

A solid workbench is extremely important. The bench shown is made of 2 x 6 framing and extremely sturdy with a large work surface covered with hardboard.

Lighting

The workbench or work space should be well lit with light directed down on the work area. A fluorescent work light suspended above the work area, but high enough you can't accidentally hit it with a gun barrel is a good choice. This provides a good even lighting without any glare on shiny metal parts.

Tool and Material Storage

You will also need lots of tool storage, including shelves for some tools and materials and a cabinet or chest for others. Purchased cabinets, shelves and racks can be used. Or you can make up your own to fit your particular tool and material storage needs. The Projects section contains plans for proper storage.

Vises

A gun vise is invaluable for holding guns for cleaning, installing scopes and other chores. The Tipton Best Gun Vise has a host of features. It accommodates bolt-action rifles, break-open shotguns, AR-15s and handguns for cleaning, maintenance and gunsmithing work. A central aluminum channel allows the individual components to move into the perfect position for every firearm. The rear base features two independently adjustable offset clamps for a tight grip on a wide range of buttstock configurations. Trays for holding bottles, parts and cleaning rods are directly molded into the base.

A solid, swiveling machinist's vise is a necessity for a lot of gun work. These are not cheap, but sometimes can be picked up secondhand. They should be bolted securely on one end of a workbench so you can use it for vertical as well as horizontal work. These vises often come with serrated steel jaws, and for most gun work

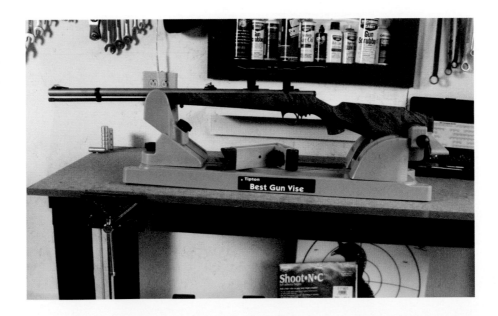

A gun vise can be extremely valuable. The Tipton gun vise shown is extremely versatile and will hold rifles as well as shotguns for cleaning and maintenance.

you'll want to pad the jaws to protect the gun finish. The pads can easily be made from scrap wood and carpeting.

In addition to the bench vises, you'll need a small pin vise for handling small screws, as well as a drill-press vise if you plan to do any extensive metalworking and milling. A set of small parallel-jaw metal clamps can be used for holding sights in place for soldering and other chores.

A solid machinist's vise is also extremely important. The Wilton Tool Vise shown swivels and has serrated jaws.

A pair of shop-made padded vise jaws can be used to protect gun finishes during vise work.

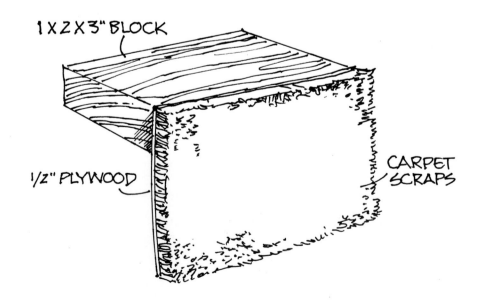

1 X 2 X 3" BLOCK

1/2" PLYWOOD

CARPET SCRAPS

GUNSMITHING TOOLS

As with many other hobbies, you can become as involved as you wish with tools. You can do a lot of gunsmithing with nothing more than a plastic and brass faced hammer, a good set of gunsmithing screwdrivers and punches, as well as a cleaning kit. Or you can have a full shop of tools, including specialty tools for working on specific guns.

One of the most common mistakes made by beginning gunsmiths is to use a standard screwdriver. These have a tapered head that often doesn't fit gun screw slots. The result is a torn-up screw head, a screw that is so damaged it can't be removed easily or worse yet, a burred and scratched receiver or other surrounding gun parts. Specialized sets of gunsmithing screwdrivers are the best bet. These come with a handle and a number of heads sized to fit gun screws. They also are hollow ground with the tips flat instead of tapered. Excellent sets are available from Brownell's as well as Wheeler.

With the Deluxe Gunsmithing Screwdriver Set from Wheeler Engineering you can have the correct bit for virtually any gunsmithing chore. Each set contains 54 flat, hollow-ground bits in different widths and thicknesses, eight Allen bits, four Phillips bits and three Torx bits. All the bits are treated to Rockwell hardness of 58-60 C. Two handle sizes are supplied with each set. A Professional set contains an additional 17 specialty bits and tools for specific gunsmithing chores, such as Smith & Wesson rebound spring tool, MI Garand rear sight adjustment tool, 1911 grip bushing driver and scope base windage bits. The sets are contained in a sturdy injection molded case.

Files are also necessary for working metal parts, smoothing burrs and other chores. You'll need a draw file for smoothing and polishing for blueing and metal finishing. You'll also find an assortment of small needle files, including a screw-head file, helpful.

One of the worst mistakes in gunsmithing is using an ordinary screwdriver for gun work. The tapered blade doesn't fit the fine head screws. A set of gunsmithing screwdrivers, such as the Wheeler Engineering 54-piece set features hollow-ground blades to match gun screws.

Other tools include files, punches, hammers, pliers, tap and die set and measuring tools.

Punches are needed for driving out pins. You'll need set of pin punches as well as roll-pin punches.

For most gun work you'll need hammers. These should include a small ball-peen or riveting hammer, a hide faced mallet or hammer, and a plastic and/or brass faced hammer. Don't use an ordinary woodworking hammer for gun work. The face is too hard and may shatter out, causing injury. In addition the face is flatter so it won't strike as well as a metal working hammer, and can mar metal surfaces.

You'll also need a hacksaw and a fine and coarse blade. Purchase only good quality blades. A variety of pliers can also be helpful, including a pair of linesman's pliers, locking pliers, flatnose and needlenose pliers as well as a pair of side-cutters. Pliers, however, are often used on guns when they shouldn't. Many fine guns have been ruined by the careless use of pliers. In addition to a small measuring tape and a soft tape, a vernier caliper that takes both inside and outside measurements can be extremely handy.

Taps and Dies

One of the most important tools for the serious gunsmith is a good set of standard size taps and dies. A special set made up just for gunsmithing is the best choice as they have the sizes most often needed for gun work. You will need at least a set of 6 x 48 taps in carbon or high-speed steel for scope work. The hardened-steel receivers are best tapped using a tap-holding jig such as that from B-Square Co. It fits in your drill press. In use the receiver is held in place on your drill press table with a drill press jig. The hole is bored, then the jig fits into the drill press collet and the tap is automatically aligned properly. Tap and screw extractors can save lots of headaches and problems as well.

Special gunsmithing tool kits, such as that shown from Brownell's, include the most used tools.

Tool Kits

As you progress in your projects, you'll need additional pliers, pin punches, gun picks and specialty tools. The best method of acquiring many gunsmithing tools is to purchase a kit. The Brownell's Basic Gunsmithing Kit has 24 tools plus 6 additional screwdriver bits to help you do basic repairs. It includes: parallel pliers, nylon/brass hammer, screwdriver kit, instrument screwdrivers, main-spring vise, India stone, brush, pin punches, starter punch, replacement pin punch set and nylon/brass drift pin punch set, bench knife, hand cut files, chain nose pliers, hand rasp, scribe hook, Allen wrench set, screw checker and box to hold all the tools.

Wheeler Engineering, from Battenfeld Technologies, also has a Basic Gunsmithing Kit that gets you started with the basic tools.

They also offer a 30-piece assembly/disassembly tool kit for more professional work. And, if you get into repairing specific guns, you can also purchase, for instance, a 41-piece tool kit just for Smith & Wesson revolvers.

Wheeler Engineering, from Battenfeld Technologies, also has a Basic Gunsmithing Kit. Their tool kit was chosen by gunsmiths and includes: space saver screwdriver kit, hammer, stainless gunsmith pick set, 8-piece steel punch set, M16 brush, dial calipers, long-nose pliers, India stone, brass drift pin, mini-screwdriver set, cleaning brush, magnifier, needle-nose pliers set, surgical tubing and a smooth-cut, 6" hand file.

Stock Tools

Woodcarving and wood shaping tools are also necessary for shaping stocks and other woodworking chores. This includes wood rasps and rifflers in a variety of shapes and sizes. The Stanley Surform tools along with a standard flat-round cabinet rasp can make quick work of stock shaping. A good set of woodcarving chisels can also make the initial roughing-in of a stock much easier. You can purchase these in a set, but the most commonly used include: a straight 18mm gouge, long bent 18mm gouge, straight 2mm parting tool, straight 10mm patternmaker's chisel and a 10mm patternmaker's gouge. A set of ordinary woodworking chisels can also be helpful. And, you'll need a tapered stone for honing the gouges and a good straight stone for straight chisels. A wooden mallet and rawhide mallet completes the basic woodcarving tool set.

One of the most common gunsmithing woodworking chores is inletting a stock for a barrel. Or in some cases you may be creating a stock from "scratch." In any case a number of tools are made for shaping the barrel channel of a stock. Brownell's handles a full line of inletting tools, including barrel bedding tools in several sizes to

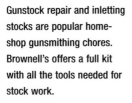

Gunstock repair and inletting stocks are popular home-shop gunsmithing chores. Brownell's offers a full kit with all the tools needed for stock work.

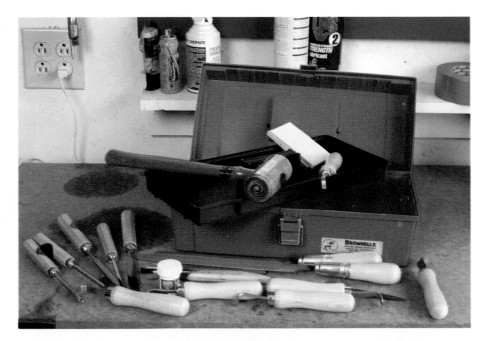

match specific barrel sizes. To use these, the two-handed tools are pulled along the barrel channel to "shave" off materials. Brownell's also has their hard-fit curl scrapers in a variety of shapes. These tools are not intended for roughing out barrel channels. They curl off the tiniest of slivers for precise fitting and are available in curved as well as straight cutting edges. The latter are perfect for inletting octagon barrels. There are also special octagon barrel bedding tools as well. You'll also need inletting black or Prussian blue paste. These are applied to the parts being fitted and when brought together, any "high spots" will be clearly marked. A set of stockmaker's hand screws are extremely handy. These are used for the final fitting of the stock to the action and their T-shaped handles make it easy to quickly install and remove the action when fitting.

As with many tools, complete kits are also available. Brownell's offers their Stockmaker's Starter Kit. This comprehensive collection of the proper chisels, files, gouges, scrapers and other tools allows you to turn a rough-cut, semi-inletted blank into a personal, beautiful work of art. The Brownell's Tech Support Staff selected the tools especially to give you just what you need in a wide selection of professional quality tools. As your skill and expertise improves, you can add other tools later. The Stockmaker's Advanced Tool Kit includes Henckel chisels and gouges, inletting black, acid brushes, hand carving knife, files and file handles, curl scraper kit, Quickut inletting tool, patternmaker's rasp, rawhide mallet, hard felt pads and sandpaper.

Checkering Tools

One of the most fascinating woodworking projects for the gun tinkerer is checkering. Of course, you'll need checkering tools. You can get by with only a small veining tool,

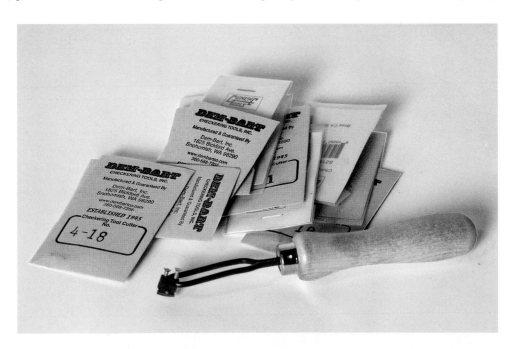

Gunstock checkering is fun and a great way of embellishing guns. Checkering tools, such as those from Brownell's, are required.

a single-line and double-line cutter, but a checkering kit is the best bet. For first-time checkering, get a set with no more than 18 lines per inch. Brownell's carries a full line of checkering tools and accessories. They also offer a Dem-Bart Starter Set for the beginner and a Master Set for the professional. The Starter Set features a No. 1C single-line cutter with handle, No. 1F cutter only, No. 2 line cutter with handle, No. 4 guide line cutter only, No. S-1 cutter only and No. B-1 border cutter. All are 90° cutters. The Master Set includes four cutters with handles to handle any checkering chore. The only additional tool you might need is a veiner. A video on checkering and a number of classic checkering patterns are also available. A full line of replacement cutters are available for use with the Dem-Bart handles.

Hobby gunsmiths are always looking for new projects and challenges; checkering, however, is one job many are afraid to tackle. The Miles Gilbert Learn to Checker Kit, from Battenfeld Technologies, contains a DVD with comprehensive,

Miles Gilbert offers a Learn to Checker Kit that contains a DVD with extensive instructions.

You will also need a checkering cradle to hold the gun. The Brownell's model shown is economical and easy to use.

detailed instructions that anyone can follow. The deluxe kit includes five ergonomic handles, five cutters (18 lines per inch), four practice coasters, circle and diamond lay-out templates, five exclusive Miles Gilbert see-through checkering guides and an easy-to-follow instructional DVD. The kit also includes five patent-pending alignment guides that make it easy to cut crisp, true lines.

You can also make your own checkering tools. They can be shaped of mild tool steel rod, ground and shaped as desired. Wooden handles can be carved or turned on a lathe. Information on making your own checkering tools is in the Projects section.

You will also need a checkering cradle for working on rifle stocks, as well as shotgun stocks and forearms. Handgun grips can be screwed to a wooden block held in a rotating craft-vise. Both Brownell's and Miles Gilbert offer checkering cradles. You can also make up your own checkering cradle quite easily. One is featured in the Projects section.

Cleaning Tools

The most common gun chore is cleaning and it's also one of the most important. You can purchase separate cleaning tools and supplies, but a number of gun cleaning tools, supplies and even kits are available that offer everything needed. I've used Birchwood Casey Products for many years and their new Synthetic Safe Cleaner Gun Scrubber is a gun cleaning solvent that can be used on all guns, including those with synthetic stocks. They also offer Bore Scrubber, Sheath Rust Preventive and cleaning cloths, black powder solvent and other supplies. Other cleaning solvents and supplies are available from Blue Wonder Gun Care Products, Shooters Choice and KG Industries.

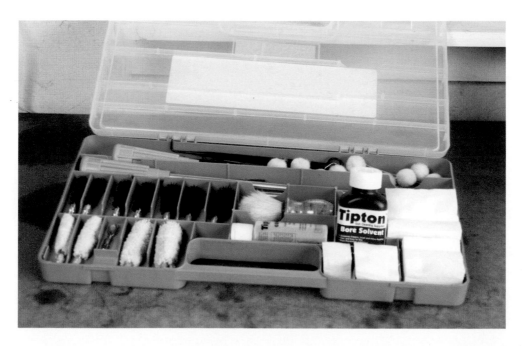

Gun cleaning is probably the most common chore. A wide range of cleaning tools and materials are available. You can purchase separately, or in complete kits, such as the Battenfeld Technologies Tipton Shotgun Cleaning Kit shown.

Battenfeld Technologies Tipton has a full line of cleaning supplies and kits. The Shotgun Cleaning Kit contains 7 bore/chamber brushes, 4 bore mops, 200 patches, shotgun patch puller, utility brush, nylon gun brush, 10 shooter's swabs, 3 ounce bore solvent, 2 ounce gun oil, 4 cleaning picks, 3-piece cleaning rod and a chamber rod. All is contained in a handy see-through case. The Tipton Range Box with Complete Rifle/Handgun Cleaning Kit consists of a sturdy case with a removable cleaning kit. It also has a rubberized cradle to hold the firearm. The big box also has compartmentalized storage space, and is a solvent resistant polymer construction. The cleaning kit, which is also available separately, contains: 11 bronze brushes, 12 brass jags, 4 slotted tips, 200 patches (22–45 calibers), utility brush, nylon gun brush, 3-piece cleaning rod (22 caliber), 10 shooter's swabs, 3 ounce bore solvent, 2 ounce gun oil, action/chamber cleaning tool set, 4 cleaning picks and 3-piece cleaning rod (27–45 calibers).

If purchasing separate cleaning tools, make sure you acquire the proper-size tool to fit your caliber or gauge gun. Cleaning rods may be jointed aluminum or wood, which are often used for shotguns, but steel rods should be used for cleaning rifles. Aluminum rods shouldn't be used for cleaning rifles because most aren't strong enough and may bend from the pressure needed to force the proper-size cleaning brushes through the barrel. A number of different types of cleaning rod tips are also available including the slotted patch tip, brush, jag tip for patches and swabs.

Scope Installation Tools

Installing a scope on a rifle is another project that's fairly easy. In addition to a gun vise and the proper screws, you'll also need a bore sighter. The Simmons model is fairly inexpensive and easy to use. The LaserLyte's Universal Laser Bore Sighter can also be used to mount a scope or check the sights after arriving in hunting camp.

Installing a rifle scope is another very common and easy project. Specialized scope mounting tools are available. After the scope is mounted it should be bore sighted. The LaserLyte Universal Bore Sighter uses a laser for quick work.

A solid, steady gun rest is important for the sighting in of guns. The Caldwell Lead Sled also provides a means of reducing recoil during sight-in.

A gun rest is also a good idea for sighting-in scopes and iron sights. Caldwell's Rock BR is a quality front rest that can help in holding the gun for scope sight-in or testing rifle and ammunition performance. The ultimate for sighting-in and testing, however, is the Caldwell Lead Sled. You can add weight to the rest to reduce recoil. There is more weightless recoil, with up to 95 percent recoil reduction. This is great for magnum rifles and testing slug guns. Made of durable welded construction, it features a sled that will hold up to four 25-pound bags of lead shot. It has rear elevation adjustment, fingertip front elevation adjustment and rubber feet.

Just as important as a sturdy, stable shooting table or bench, is something solid to support your gun. Battenfeld Technologies Caldwell has a couple of gun steady rests that are easy to transport and easy to set up yet provide solid shooting rests. The Caldwell Steady Rest is built of polymer material and features front and rear bags as an integral part of the rest. The front rest is adjustable from 8$^{1}/_{2}$–11" and will accommodate forends up to 2$^{1}/_{8}$". Features include a built-in handle for easy transport and a convenient tray for holding shooting and cleaning supplies. If you're looking for a lightweight, easy-to-transport rest, the Handy Rest features an improved, soft, over-molded cradle that allows convenient shooting without the use of sand-filled bags. The large knob provides quick and easy height adjustment. To add to the convenience, Caldwell Shooting Supplies also has Insta View Targets. You no longer have to walk down range to see where your bullets are striking the target. Upon impact, the black coating flakes off around each bullet hole, leaving a bright, fluorescent yellow ring. The Birchwood Casey Shoot-N-C Self-Adhesive Bull's-Eye Targets offer the same technology.

Power Tools

Any number of power tools can also be a great help. A small bench grinder is one of the most important. It can be used to regrind tool faces and edges, or to make small parts. Fitted with a wire wheel it can be used to remove rust and smooth up metal parts. In addition, cloth wheels can be fitted to spindle grinders and when used with abrasive

A small bench grinder can be used for shaping of gun parts.

A belt grinder can also be used for minor shaping.

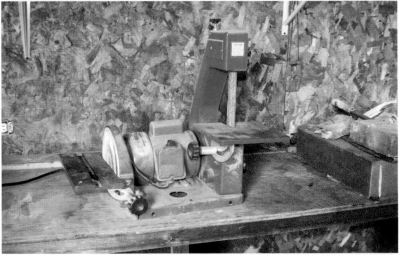

A Dremel tool can be invaluable for inletting and smoothing small parts.

sticks, can be used for polishing metal. Another type of grinder is a belt grinder. The belt can be used to sharpen tools, and it doesn't heat up the metal as quickly as does a wheel grinder. The small flat table in front of the belt allows you to hold small parts with a pair of locking pliers for grinding and shaping. With a coarse belt, the sander can also be used for rough shaping of gunstocks. A dedicated wood disc/belt sander does a better job with these chores. This tool is especially handy for installing recoil pads. You can cut down the recoil pad at the same time you shape the stock. Or fit to the outline of a finished stock. A small hand grinder such as a Dremel-Moto Tool with accessories is also extremely handy. It can't be beat for fast shaping of inletted areas, as well as for grinding and polishing small metal parts.

A propane or gas torch can be used for everything from soldering and heat-treating to blueing small parts such as screws. Most gun metal joining is done by brazing or silver soldering and a small welding-torch is handy for these chores. For larger chores a wire-feed welder is the best choice.

Drill bits are a necessity. Make sure you purchase only good quality bits, and keep a drill-bit and screw-thread gauge on hand.

Safety goggles or a face shield are also necessary, and a lighted magnifier can be handy for working intricate parts in place.

Specialized Tools

In addition to the tools listed, a number of specialized tools have evolved that can help do a specific job better. There is no need to purchase these tools until you have a specific need for them. A barrel-sight drill jig consists

A propane torch can be used for soldering and brazing chores.

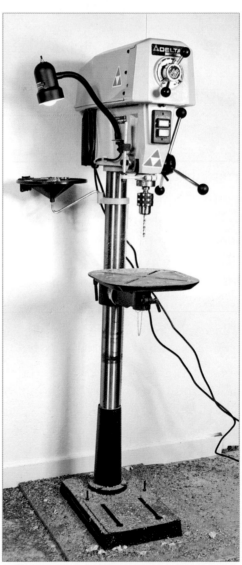

A drill press and bits is a major investment but a great helpmate.

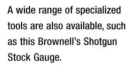

A wide range of specialized tools are also available, such as this Brownell's Shotgun Stock Gauge.

of a V-block guide to ensure boring precision holes in rifle barrels and shotgun ramps for installing front bead sights. A shotgun sight installer is a small gripping tool that enables you to quickly and easily install a bead sight on a gun without damaging the surrounding metal. A rib sight jig can be used to locate and bore the holes in a rib on a single or double-barrel shotgun. When inletting bolt actions, you'll do a lot of assembling and disassembling to fit the action properly in place. Guard screw wrenches are quicker than using the guard screws from the action and prevent tearing up the guard screws with constant use during the fitting. A scope-mounting tool has a large screw head for mounting scopes on the bases and has more leverage than a screwdriver. It prevents marring and burring the mounts. A front sight pusher makes it easy to remove and install front sights without marring the surrounding metal.

When fitting a shotgun stock, a gunstock gauge can provide an accurate measurement. The Brownell's gauge measures the stock pull and the drop at the heel. When removing a barrel from the action, a barrel vice and action wrench makes it easier to hold the barrel and turn off the action. If you get into choking and working on shotgun barrels, a Shotgun Choking Kit from Brownell's includes reamers, barrel calipers and a barrel hone. For true choke work you should also have chamber reamers. These are used first, the gun patterned and then the choke alteration work done. A swivel jig and drill set guides the bit on the gunstock, then can be turned upside down to go into the barrel channel to bore the front swivel hole. The drill set has a locking collar that stops bits at the correct depth and prevents boring through the barrel channel. A lot of gun work involves working tiny, delicate pieces and several shop tweezers can be a great help.

Granted, you're probably not going to acquire all these tools and supplies at once, and you don't need to. Start simple with gunsmithing, doing cleaning and simple repairs or chores such as mounting scopes. Then add the tools as you learn more advanced chores. A home gunshop can be a pleasurable and profitable place.

Large Bench with Storage

The extremely sturdy bench shown is deep enough to hold storage shelves and a storage box on the back and has drawers and a bottom shelf for additional storage. With a heavy-duty vise on one end it will handle even the toughest of gun chores. The bench is 36" high, the normal height of kitchen countertops. If you're tall, you might wish to add an inch or so. The lower shelf is big enough to hold bench rests, and other bulky items, yet is set back so you can also sit at the bench on a tall stool. The bench shown is extremely sturdy, so you can hammer, pry and do many of those tough chores without movement of the bench. With the heavy-duty vise mounted on one corner, I've even found the major chore of pulling stuck muzzleloader balls quite easy. A $\frac{1}{4}$" hardboard top cover provides a very smooth top that can be replaced if it becomes damaged. The bench features simple drawers that can be used to hold tools, cleaning supplies, scopes and gunsmithing parts.

The bench can be constructed with just a few tools including a portable circular saw, carpenter's square and tape measure. You can assemble with

The large workbench shown has lots of storage space, a large worktop and is extremely sturdy.

nails and in that case you'll need a hammer. A better choice is to use self-starting wood screws to create a sturdier, longer-lasting bench. In this case, an impact driver makes the chore quick and easy.

Materials

Qty.	Part	Dimensions
4	Legs	2 x 6 x 35"
4	Leg braces	2 x 4 x 35"
4	Horizontals, side	2 x 6 x 33"
2	Horizontals, back	2 x 6 x 72"
1	Horizontal, front	2 x 4 x 72"
3	Inside top supports	2 x 4 x 33"
1	Bottom front support	2 x 6 x 69"
1	Bottom center support	2 x 6 x 17"
1	Bottom, $\frac{3}{4}$" plywood	20 x 72"
2	Drawer casing ends, $\frac{3}{4}$" plywood	24 x 36"
6	Drawer supports	$\frac{1}{2}$ x 1 x 34"
3	Drawer spacers	$\frac{3}{4}$ x $\frac{3}{4}$ x 13$\frac{1}{2}$"
1	Back, $\frac{1}{4}$" plywood	30 x 72"
1	Top, $\frac{3}{4}$" plywood	36 x 72"
1	Top cover, $\frac{1}{4}$" hardboard	36 x 72"
2	Top trim, ends	$\frac{3}{4}$ x 2$\frac{1}{2}$ x 37$\frac{1}{2}$"
2	Top trim, front and back	$\frac{3}{4}$ x 2$\frac{1}{2}$ x 71"
2	Drawer sides	$\frac{3}{4}$ x 2$\frac{1}{2}$ x 34$\frac{1}{2}$"
2	Drawer front and back	$\frac{3}{4}$ x 2$\frac{1}{2}$ x 13$\frac{1}{2}$"
2	Drawer sides	$\frac{3}{4}$ x 3$\frac{1}{2}$ x 13$\frac{1}{2}$"
2	Drawer front and back	$\frac{3}{4}$ x 3$\frac{1}{2}$ x 13$\frac{1}{2}$"
2	Drawer sides	$\frac{3}{4}$ x 4$\frac{1}{2}$ x 13$\frac{1}{2}$"
2	Drawer front and back	$\frac{3}{4}$ x 4$\frac{1}{2}$ x 13$\frac{1}{2}$"
2	Drawer sides	$\frac{3}{4}$ x 5$\frac{1}{2}$ x 13$\frac{1}{2}$"
2	Drawer front and back	$\frac{3}{4}$ x 5$\frac{3}{4}$ x 13"
4	Drawer bottoms, $\frac{1}{4}$" hardboard	15 x 36"

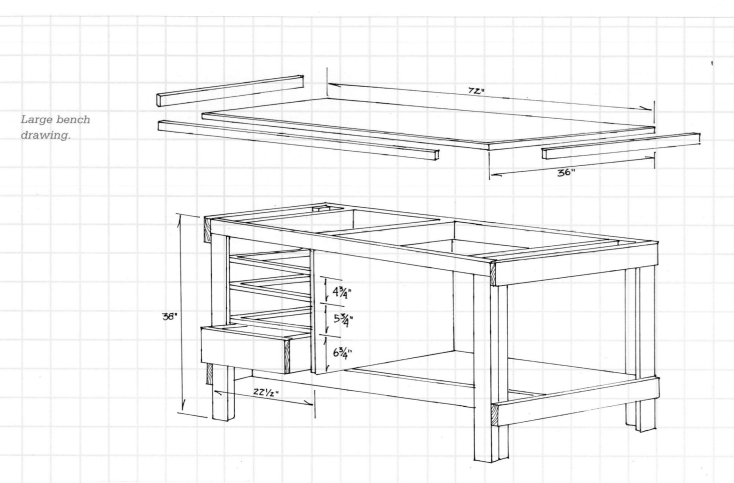

Large bench drawing.

First step is to measure for the legs and leg braces, mark a square line across the boards with a carpenter's square, then cut to length. Fasten each leg brace to a leg, creating the L-shaped leg assemblies.

Fasten the side horizontals to the outside of the leg assemblies, making sure the construction is square. Stand these leg assemblies with their backs up and fasten the two back horizontals in place. Again, make sure the assembly is square. Turn the construction over and fasten the top front horizontal in place. Then install the bottom front horizontal support, fastening between the two lower side horizontals.

Cut the bottom center support and fasten between the bottom front support and lower back horizontal. Cut the bottom to size, notching around the back legs. Fasten in place to the front and center bottom supports as well as to the back and side lower horizontals.

Cut the inside top supports and install them. Cut the drawer casing ends and install them in place. Cut the drawer supports and install them on the inside of the drawer casings. Cut the drawer front spacers and fasten them to the front edge of the appropriate drawer supports.

Cut the plywood top to the correct size and install it in place. Then cut the hardboard top cover and fasten it down. Make sure the fasteners are slightly countersunk so they don't protrude above the top. This top can also be glued down with panel adhesive for a smoother surface, but this will make it harder to replace in the future. Cut the front and back trim boards and fasten in place. Then cut the side trim boards and fasten to the top, side horizontals and into the ends of the front and back trim boards. Cut the back to fit between the lower back horizontals and fasten it to the outside of the rear legs.

The next step is to create the drawers. Cut both sides, front and back for the top drawer, then cut the sides, front and back for the next lower drawer, then the next and finally the bottom drawer. Fasten the drawer sides, fronts and backs together to create the drawers. Then cut the drawer bottoms and fasten them on the bottom of each drawer. When fastening the drawer bottoms in place, make sure the drawers are square.

Install the knobs on the drawers and slide them in place. The bench can be left as is, or given a coat of clear finish to protect it, or painted.

Simple Gunsmithing Bench

Regardless of whether you do nothing more than clean your guns, simple chores such as adding a rifle scope, or do more advanced gunsmithing, a good, solid workbench is a must. The bench shown has all those qualities and more, but is less complicated to build than the previous bench. Again, a smooth top makes it easy to pick up and work with small pieces. A Columbia woodworking vise on one end and bench vise on the opposite provide a means of holding a variety of parts and guns for different chores. Slots in one end hold cleaning rods for easy access. A sturdy shelf on the bottom holds large items. Many gunsmithing chores require a bench that is sturdy and won't rock or move when doing vise work. The bench shown features doubled 2 x 4 legs which makes it also an ideal bench for holding a reloader and supplies. The bench shown is also made of readily available common materials and is fairly easy to build. In fact, you can build it with nothing more than a portable circular saw, saber saw or hand saw, square, tape measure and cordless

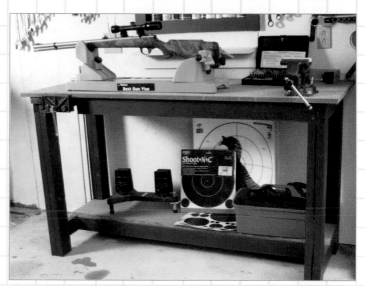

The simple workbench shown is made of standard 2 x 4 material with a 3/4" MDF top and shelf. It's easily made, yet quite sturdy.

drill/driver. If you're somewhat handy you can probably build this bench in a weekend.

Materials

		2 x 4 x 35$\frac{1}{4}$"	
B	2	Front and back top supports	2 x 4 x 55"
C	2	Top end supports	2 x 4 x 22"
D	1	Back shelf support	2 x 4 x 53"
E	1	Front shelf support	2 x 4 x 56"
F	4	Bottom leg cleats	2 x 4 x 4"
G	4	Upper leg cleats	2 x 4 x 4"
H	1	Shelf, $\frac{3}{4}$ MDF	13 x 59"
I	1	Top, $\frac{3}{4}$ MDF	24 x 63"
		Self-starting wood screws	2$\frac{1}{2}$"and 1$\frac{1}{2}$"

The first step is to cut the inside 2 x 4 legs (A). Note the bench shown is designed with a 36" working height, a typical kitchen counter height. Depending on your stature or whether you prefer to stand or sit while working, you may wish to raise or lower this height. Cut notches in the top edges of the legs to accept the front and back top supports. Cut the front and back top supports (B) to length. Fasten the top supports to the front and back of the inside legs with their ends down in the notches. Use 2$\frac{1}{2}$" self-starting wood screws countersinking them below the wood surface. Make

sure the assembly is square. Hold a carpenter's square against the edge while driving the screws in place. With both front and back inside leg assemblies constructed, stand them upside down on a smooth, flat surface. Cut and fasten the top end supports (C) in place, again making sure the assembly is square. Cut and fasten the back shelf support (D) in place between the two back legs with 3" screws driven in from the outside of the inside legs. Stand the assembly upright on a smooth, flat surface and make sure it sits squarely and doesn't rock. Then cut and fasten the lower

Simple Gunsmithing Bench cont'd

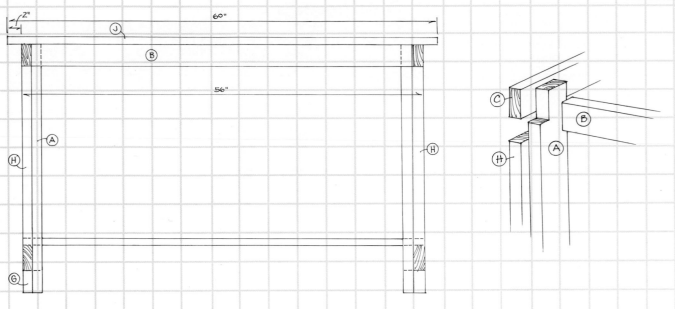

Simple bench detail drawings.

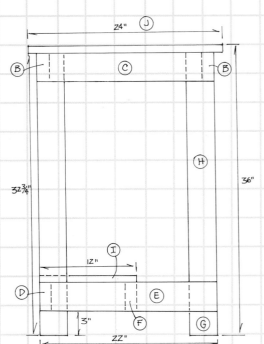

end/shelf supports (E) to the outside of the inside legs
as well. Note these must be at the same location on the
legs as the back shelf support. Cut and fasten the front
shelf support (E) in place between the lower end/shelf
supports. The legs are strengthened by adding 2 x 4
cleats to the inside legs. Cut the bottom short cleats,
drill starting holes in them using the countersink bit
and fasten in place below the lower end/shelf supports.
Cut the upper cleats to length and fasten them in place
in the same manner. If you wish to paint the frame now
is a good time to do so as you can more easily get to
the inside surfaces.

Cut the bottom shelf board to size from medium
density fiberboard (MDF) or if you prefer, cut from
solid-faced plywood. The MDF provides a stronger,
smoother, more easily cleaned surface. The best
method of cutting this heavy material is to lay it on a
pair of sawhorses or other flat surface, lay a couple of
scrap pieces beneath the board, set a portable circular
saw to cut about $1/8$" below the wood surface. Use a
straight edge to mark the cut, and then saw with a
portable electric circular saw. Note the back corners
will have to be cut to fit around the back legs. Mark
these cuts using a square, then use a saber saw or
hand saw to make the cuts. Install the shelf board
down on the front and back shelf supports and the

lower end/shelf supports. Fasten in place with $1\frac{1}{2}$"
countersunk self-starting wood screws.

Cut the top in the same manner. If you are installing a wood vise such as the one shown, you will
need to notch for the vise threads to go through the
front top support. You should also add a support brace
to the area. The top will also have to be notched to fit
around the back side of the wood vise. Make these
cuts, try-fit the vise and top before fastening the top
securely in place. Note the top protrudes 1" around all

Left photo, notches cut in the top of the workbench are used to hold cleaning rods. Top right, the notches in the top of the legs are easily cut with a bandsaw. Center right, self-starting wood screws and glue are used to assemble the bench. Make sure it is assembled square. Lower right, then the vise is mounted to the bench top.

sides. Then position the top in place and fasten securely to the top supports with 1½" self-starting wood screws. Just lightly countersink these so they don't leave a deep depression. If installing the metal-working vise, locate it in position and mark the anchor holes. Note the front holes are located directly over the front support. Anchor the front of the vise in place with ⅜ x 3" lag screws. Anchor the rear holes to the top with ⅜ x 2" carriage bolts and nuts.

The final step is to cut the notches to accept the cleaning rods. Determine the diameter of your rods

and bore a hole down through the overhanging lip of the bench top near the outside edge of the top support for each rod. Then use the square to mark a cut line on either side of the hole out to the top edge. Make these cuts with a saber or hand saw. If you wish, you can add a clear finish to the MDF top and shelf board.

Now it's time to really do some cleaning on that rifle or shotgun you have been neglecting for some time. You'll find all your gunsmithing chores easier with your new bench.

Tool and Material Storage

The tool shelf shown with the first workbench is designed specifically to hold the most used gun tools, including pliers, screwdrivers, gun picks and drift pins as well as cleaning and refinishing supplies.

A tool chest designed much like a machinist's chest holds parts and less used tools. Begin construction by cutting the sides, top, bottom and back to size. Cut $\frac{1}{4}$ x $\frac{1}{4}$" rabbets in the back edges of the sides, top and bottom. Lay the sides next to each other and mark the location of the wooden drawer slides using a carpenter's square. Rip the drawer slides to $\frac{3}{4}$" from $\frac{3}{4}$" stock and install them in place on the sides with glue and brads, or using crown staples and an air nailer. Fasten the sides to the top and bottom with glue and self-starting wood screws. Cut and fasten the back in

place with glue and brads or crown staples. Rip the front drawer supports from $\frac{3}{4}$" stock, cut them to fit and install with glue and self-starting wood screws.

The drawers are constructed of $\frac{3}{4}$" stock with $\frac{1}{4}$" bottoms set in $\frac{1}{4}$ x $\frac{1}{4}$" rabbets in the front, and sides, and $\frac{1}{4}$" up from their bottom edges. The back is cut $\frac{1}{2}$" narrower than the sides and front. The drawer bottom fits over the back. Rip the drawer pieces to the correct size and cut the rabbets in them using a table saw. Fasten the front to the sides, and then fasten the back to the sides. Cut the drawer bottoms to size and install them in the rabbets. Using a square, assure the drawers are square, and then fasten the back to the bottom edge of the back using glue and brads. Add knobs or pulls as desired.

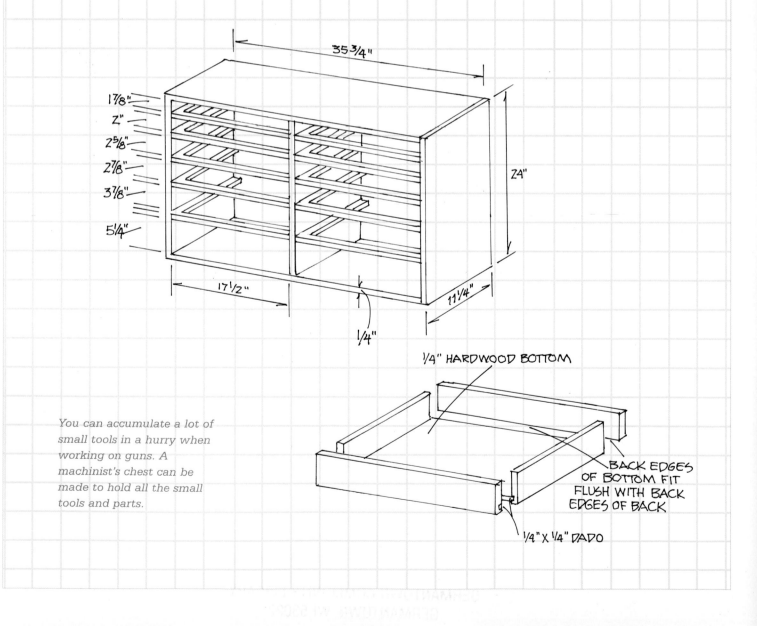

You can accumulate a lot of small tools in a hurry when working on guns. A machinist's chest can be made to hold all the small tools and parts.

Gun Support Cradle

You can also build your own gun "vise" for working on guns in your shop. The design shown doesn't clamp the gun securely in place as with commercial vises. But it does cradle the gun securely for stock work, installing scopes, cleaning and other chores. It is very easily made and constructed of standard 2 x 6 material readily available at your local building supply dealer. Scrap carpeting protects your valuable guns from scratches. First step in construction is to cut the base to length. Then cut the front support block to shape. The best tactic is to cut it 9" in length, then mark the location for the support circle, the center at 6". Cut this with a forstner bit. Then cut across the bored hole to create a 6" high support board with the half circle centered. Fasten the front support board in

place with glue and screws from the base, up into the support block.

Cut the rear support block to size and shape. Note it is tapered to allow the gun stock to slide down securely against it. Fasten in place again with glue and screws. Cut the front support block to size and shape.

You will probably want to set your favorite gun in place against the rear support block to determine the location of the front support block. Move the block in or out as desired. Once you've determined a location that will securely support your gun with both blocks, fasten the front support block in place with glue and screws. Finally, rip the bottom support strips to width and attach with glue and screws.

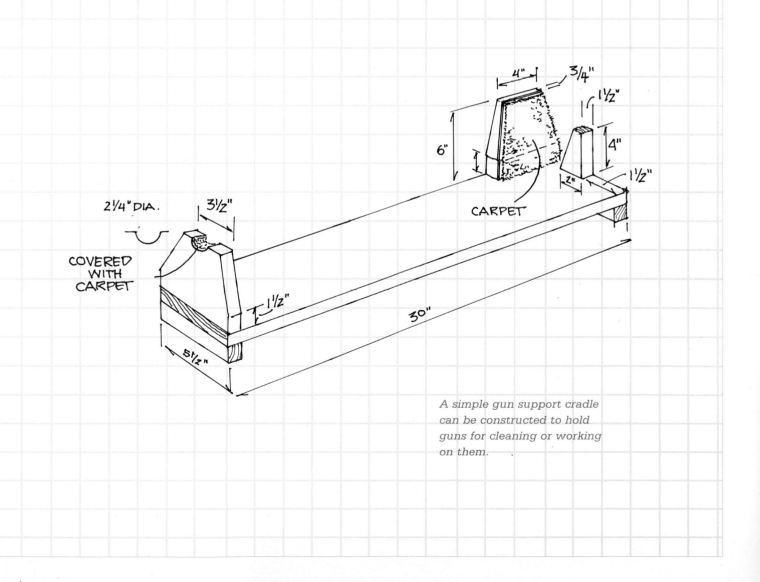

A simple gun support cradle can be constructed to hold guns for cleaning or working on them.

Checkering Cradle and Checkering Tools

A checkering cradle can also be handmade if you prefer. It is made of 1x material with a 2 x 4 block on the bottom that is clamped in a vise to position the stock as needed. Solid wood blocks are also used as fore-end and butt holders. The cradle shown has a sliding fore-end holder to adjust for a variety of stocks from rifle to shotgun.

Checkering tools can also be made of $3/16$" steel rod. Bend to the shapes shown, then grind and file the teeth in them. The handles can be carved or whittled to the shapes shown.

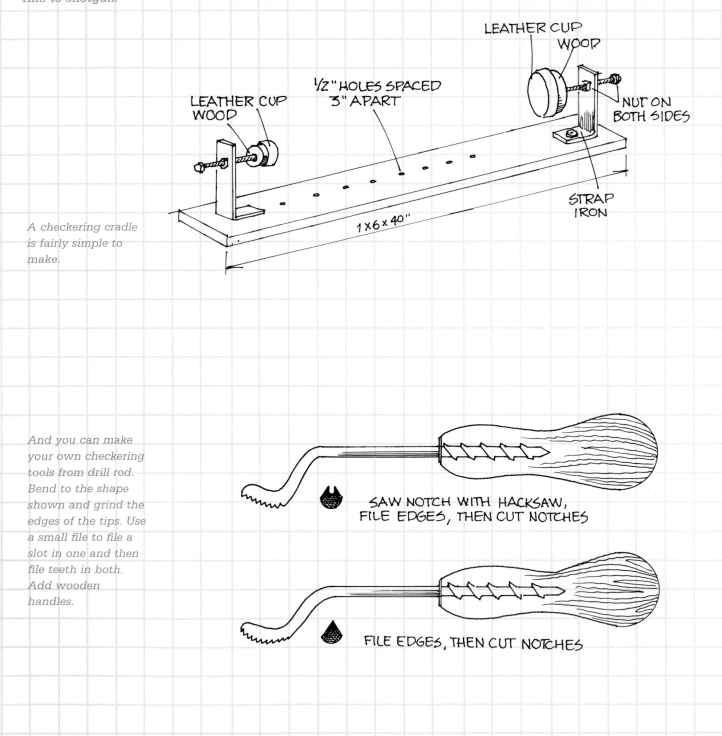

A checkering cradle is fairly simple to make.

LEATHER CUP
WOOD

½" HOLES SPACED
3" APART

LEATHER CUP
WOOD

NUT ON
BOTH SIDES

STRAP
IRON

1 X 6 X 40"

And you can make your own checkering tools from drill rod. Bend to the shape shown and grind the edges of the tips. Use a small file to file a slot in one and then file teeth in both. Add wooden handles.

SAW NOTCH WITH HACKSAW,
FILE EDGES, THEN CUT NOTCHES

FILE EDGES, THEN CUT NOTCHES

Bench Chest

A chest or box to tote supplies, such as spotting scopes, targets, ammunition and push pins for bench shooting, can be mighty handy. A large plastic tackle box will suffice, and plastic bench boxes are also available. You can also make your own quite easily. The box shown is made of $\frac{1}{2}$" solid material with a $\frac{1}{4}$" plywood bottom and top to cut down on weight. Fasten the sides to the ends with glue and brads, and then fasten the top and bottom in place with glue and brads, creating a solid box, lid and all. Set the brads below the wood surface and fill the holes with wood putty. Then sand all surfaces. Use a table saw to cut around all outside surfaces to remove the lid from the box bottom. Make sure the cut is spaced so you don't cut through any brads. Sand the cut edges smooth, and then finish to suit. The chest shown utilizes brass chest hardware. Install the hinges on the back, the catch on the front and the handle on top. You may wish to add felt or flocking to protect your spotting scope.

Materials

Qty.	Part	Dimensions
1	Front	$\frac{1}{2}$ x $5\frac{3}{4}$ x 16"
1	Back	$\frac{1}{2}$ x $5\frac{3}{4}$ x 16"
2	Ends	$\frac{1}{2}$ x $5\frac{1}{2}$ x $9\frac{1}{2}$"
1	Top	$\frac{1}{4}$ x 10 x 16"
1	Bottom	$\frac{1}{4}$ x 9 x 16"
2	Hinges	
1	Latch	
1	Handle	

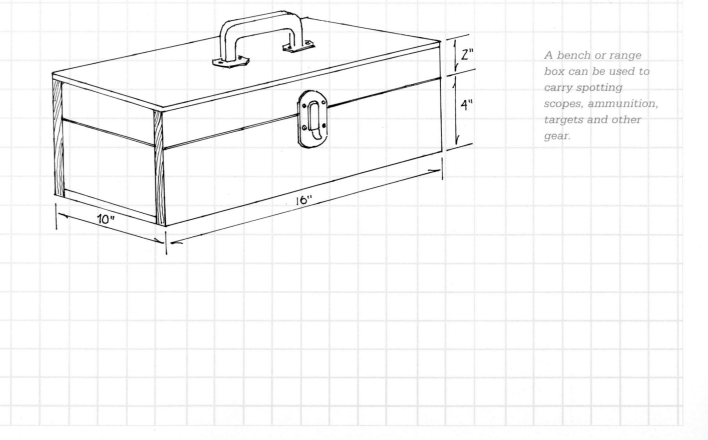

A bench or range box can be used to carry spotting scopes, ammunition, targets and other gear.

Shooting Table

Gun sight-in and bench shooting practice require a shooting table. And, the first prerequisite for a table is sturdiness. You don't want a wobbly, shaking table, or you'll end up extremely frustrated with your shooting ability and your gun won't be properly sighted-in. The table shown is made of treated 2 x 4s and 2 x 6s. You can leave it outside to weather without any problem and the table is extremely easy to build.

First step in construction is to cut all legs to size. Then cut the top and bottom stretcher to length. Fasten the stretchers to the front and back table legs using glue and self-starting wood screws. Check each leg assembly with a carpenter's square and make sure they are assembled square.

Cut the short top side stretchers to length. Stand the leg assemblies up on one side, propping them in place. Fasten one short top side stretcher in place over the leg assemblies and to the ends of the front and rear top stretchers. Cut the long bottom stretchers to length. Cut the front short legs to length. Fasten the short legs to the outer ends of the long stretchers, again making sure the joint is square. Then fasten the long leg assembly over the leg assemblies and bottom front and back stretchers.

Cut the top boards to length. Fasten in place down on the top stretchers with screws countersunk below the wood surface. Round all corners with a saber saw. Cut the bench seat boards and fasten them in place in the same manner.

A sturdy sit-down shooting table can make sight-in and other gunning chores easy and provides a good bench rest for competitive shooting.

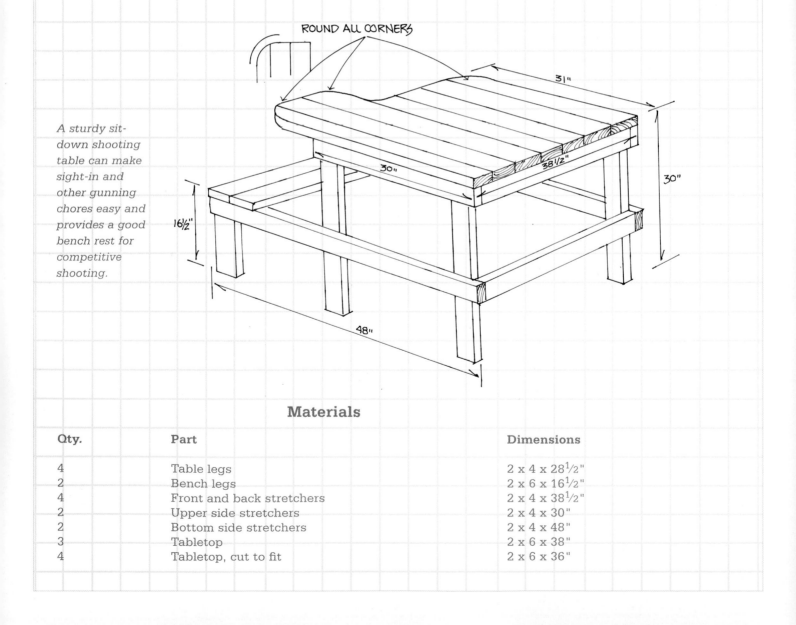

Materials

Qty.	Part	Dimensions
4	Table legs	2 x 4 x 28$\frac{1}{2}$"
2	Bench legs	2 x 6 x 16$\frac{1}{2}$"
4	Front and back stretchers	2 x 4 x 38$\frac{1}{2}$"
2	Upper side stretchers	2 x 4 x 30"
2	Bottom side stretchers	2 x 4 x 48"
3	Tabletop	2 x 6 x 38"
4	Tabletop, cut to fit	2 x 6 x 36"

Stand-Up Shooting Bench

Attending a Remington Writer's Seminar at the Bienville Plantation and testing Remington's new rifles, I had a chance to use this very effective and simple shooting bench. Rather than sitting down, this bench affords stand-up shooting which is especially effective for a gun club where several members may be lined up waiting to use a bench for sight-in, or simply for target practice. The bench is extremely comfortable, quick and easy to use. The legs are adjustable so the bench can actually be set for different heights, or even be positioned for a sit-down bench if desired or for handicapped accessibility. The bench top has arms on each side for supporting gunstocks and a cut-out in the center. This allows for left- or right-handed shooters. Or, in the case shown, two separate rifles are set up for shooting. Shelves on the bottom hold sandbags for creating a solid, wiggle-free, shooting bench.

Construction is very simple, using stock 2 x 4s and $^{3}/_{4}$" plywood. If the

A stand-up shooting bench is even easier to use, especially when a number of people are waiting to sight-in.

Materials

Qty.	Part	Dimensions
4	Bottom legs	2 x 4 x 30"
4	Top legs	2 x 4 x 30"
2	Top end aprons	2 x 4 x 18"
2	Top front and back aprons	2 x 4 x 45"
2	Bottom end aprons	2 x 4 x 24"
2	Bottom front and back aprons	2 x 4 x 45"
1	Top, $^{3}/_{4}$" plywood	36 x 48"
2	Sandbag supports, $^{3}/_{4}$" plywood	12 x 21"
16	Lag screws	$^{1}/_{4}$ x 1"
4	Implement pins	
8	Metal brackets	$1^{1}/_{2}$ x $3^{3}/_{4}$ x 3"

Stand-Up Shooting Bench cont'd

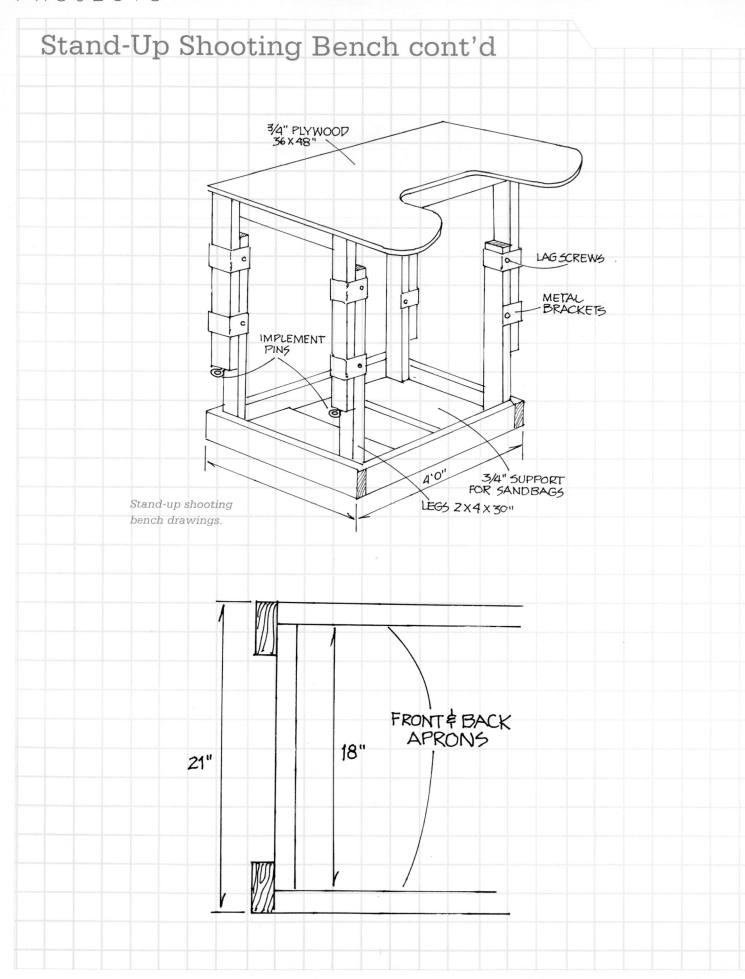

3/4" PLYWOOD
36 X 48"

LAG SCREWS

METAL
BRACKETS

IMPLEMENT
PINS

*Stand-up shooting
bench drawings.*

4'0"

3/4" SUPPORT
FOR SANDBAGS

LEGS 2 X 4 X 30"

21"

18"

FRONT & BACK
APRONS

bench is to be used outside, construct it of pressure-treated materials. The first step is to cut the 2 x 4 leg pieces to length, and then cut the 2 x 4 top aprons to length. Assemble the top framework by anchoring the top aprons to the inside edges of the legs using coated or brass, self-starting $2\frac{1}{2}$" wood screws. Make sure the leg frame is square and the legs are installed square with the frame before proceeding.

Cut the top to size, and then draw a 12 x 12" arm on each side of the top piece. Mark the cut-out between these arms. The cut-out should be 12" back from the front edge. Use a coffee can or paint can to draw the rounded outside and inside corners and then use a saber saw to cut the top arm shapes. Sand all edges and the top surface of the top smooth. Fasten the top to the top aprons using $1\frac{1}{2}$" coated or brass, self-starting wood screws down from the top into the aprons.

Cut the 2 x 4 lower legs to length. Lay the legs side-by-side with their bottom ends flush. Beginning 6" from their bottom ends, mark locations for the support pin holes. These holes should be $\frac{3}{8}$" in diameter and bored at 2" intervals. The legs are supported by clip-style implement pins and you will need four of these pins. Try to make sure the pins go easily into the holes, but are not loose enough to fall out.

The upper and lower legs are held together with sheet metal brackets, allowing the top legs to slide up and down. These sheet metal brackets can be created fairly easily. If you purchase 4" wide x 7" pieces, simply cut to fit. Or you can cut 4" wide sheet metal into the lengths needed using a hacksaw. Grind or file all cut edges and corners smooth. Holes are bored in the back edges of the brackets in order to fasten them to the inside or bottom legs. These holes can be bored with a metal bit in a portable electric drill. Mark the locations for the holes using a sheet-metal punch and for ease in starting the drill bit. Then clamp the metal piece to a solid work surface and with the drill running at a low speed, bore the holes. The clamp prevents the metal from spinning when the bit goes through. The best method is to use a drill press with the metal pieces clamped to the drill press table. The brackets must also be bent to fit around the outside or top legs. The simplest method of bending is to mark the location of the bracket bends with a sharp nail or pencil. Place one end in a vise with the mark at the top edge of the vise and then bend the metal over to form a 90° angle. Use a large hammer to assist with the bend. Place a 2 x 4 in the vise with about 6" protruding. Make the second bend over the 2 x 4, again using a hammer to assist and bending at the second bend mark.

Fasten the bottom apron pieces to the bottom legs and to each other utilizing $2\frac{1}{2}$" coated or brass, self-starting wood screws. Make sure the bottom leg frame is square and the legs are installed square with the frame. Cut the bottom sandbag support boards, notching them to fit around the upright bottom legs. Fasten in place with 2" coated or brass, self-starting deck screws driven through the aprons into the edges of the boards.

Sand smooth all the edges and corners and then paint or stain all surfaces. Place implement pins in the selected holes. With a helper, position the top assembly down over the bottom assembly with the top and bottom legs aligning. Use C-clamps to temporarily fasten all four leg assemblies together. Place a sheet metal bracket in position 3" up from the bottom of one top leg. Use $\frac{1}{4}$ x 1" lag screws to anchor the sheet metal brackets to the inside or bottom leg through the holes previously drilled. Make sure the bracket doesn't fit so tightly the legs can't slide and then position another bracket 6" above the lower bracket and fasten it in place in the same manner. Repeat the steps for the other three legs. Again, make sure the brackets are not so tight the upper legs can't slide through them easily and then adjust the height as desired by shifting the implement pins.

Now you're ready to add sandbags and shooting rests and have fun.

Shooting, Sighting-In Shed

One of the most needed and appreciated items for most gun enthusiasts is a shooting and sighting-in area. This often consists of simply sturdy tables and chairs, sandbags and a good backstop. I have, however, seen some much fancier and better set-ups at different lodges and camps I've visited. One of the best I've seen is the shooting shelter at Bienville Plantation near White Springs, Florida. I've experienced the shelter during several Remington Press Introductions and thought it would make a good project for this book.

Shooting shelters offer a lot of advantages. First is shelter from the sun and weather. This not only makes it easier to sight-in guns just prior to the hunting season, but is more conducive to year-round shooting, a good way of extending the fun. The shelter also provides a means of protecting the shooting benches, which can be left permanently in place. You can also build in a small gear storage shed on one end if desired, a place to lock up targets, sandbags and other items.

The shed shown is very simple, using standard pole-barn style construction. It is an open shed, 14' between poles front to back and 36' long. It can be made as long or short as desired. The materials must be pressure-treated or other long-lasting, insect and

A sighting-in shed with a roof over it is great for competitive shooting or gun club.

Materials

Qty.	Part	Dimensions
4	Front posts	4 x 4" x 12'
4	Rear posts	4 x 4" x 10'
10	Rafters	2 x 6" x 16'
27	Purlins	2 x 4" x 12'
6	Beams	2 x 8" x 12'
16	Bracing	2 x 6" x 4'
10	Roofing, metal and/or translucent panels	16' with lap to 36"
	Concrete to suit	2 x 6" x 4'

moisture resistant woods. All fasteners must be galvanized or other exterior fasteners.

The first step is to lay out the building. Use small wooden stakes to locate the corners and positions of the support posts. To make sure the building is square, measure diagonally from corner stake to corner stake. The diagonal measurements should be the same. If they aren't, move the stakes until the measurements are the same. Another method is to use a string line and the triangle method to establish a square outline of the building. Measure 3' on one corner string and 4' on the adjoining leg of the triangle. Measure diagonally between the two. This measurement should be 5'. If not, move the strings until the measurement is 5'. That corner is then square. Repeat for the other corners.

Place stakes at each pole location and then dig the holes. The holes should be deep enough to be below frost level in your area. Check with local Extension offices or building supply dealers as to the depth needed in your specific area and/or soil type. The holes can be dug with a hand post-hole, powered digger, or even a post-hole digger on a tractor.

In most instances the posts should be set in concrete. The simplest method of doing this is using premixed, bagged concrete, although you can mix your own from Portland cement, gravel and sand. It will normally take from two to three premixed bags per post in most locations. Pour about a 3" layer of dry mix or gravel in the bottom of the hole, pack tightly and position a post in place. Use a 4' level and plumb the post in all directions. Use 2 x 4 braces to brace the post in the plumb position. The simplest method is then to simply dump the dry mix around the post. Pour a little water around the dry mix and allow it to "set." To speed up the process, mix the premix with water, pour it around the posts and allow it to set and cure before proceeding with the shed. Repeat for all posts.

Once the posts have all set solidly, fasten the top beams to the front and back. Fasten the rafters down on the beams using joist hangers. Add the fascia board to the front and back and then fasten all bracing in place. Add the purlins over the joists, and then install the roofing of your choice. The roofing shown is metal; translucent roofing panels from Suntuf can also be utilized. Paint the framing as desired. Gravel can be used as a "floor" but the shelter shown had a concrete floor and it provides good, solid, safe footing and a support for the shooting benches.

Build a shooting shelter for your family or hunting group and you'll be able to enjoy it year-round. The shelter shown can also be scaled down lengthwise to create a "backyard" shelter as well. A shelter 16' long will more than suffice for two shooting stations and provide plenty of shade and shelter.

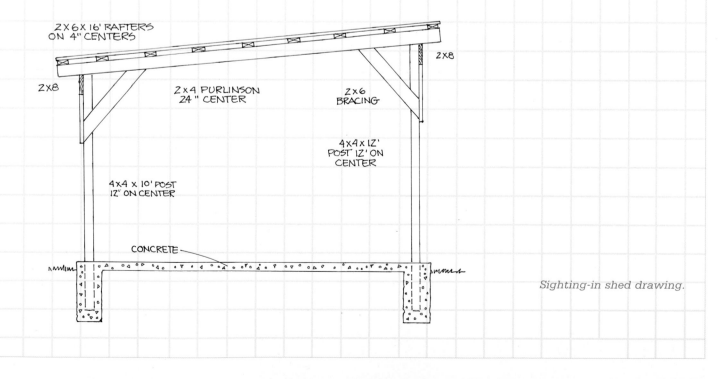

2 X 6 X 16' RAFTERS
ON 4" CENTERS

2 x 8

2 x 4 PURLINSON
24 " CENTER

2 x 6
BRACING

2 x 8

4 x 4 x 12'
POST 12' ON
CENTER

4x4 x 10' POST
12' ON CENTER

CONCRETE

Sighting-in shed drawing.

Fishing Tackle Storage

Because of the tremendous variety of fish species, techniques, tackle and gear, fishing tackle repair, building and storage can take many directions. For instance, the purist seeking trout with a fly rod will have different storage and equipment needs than a tournament bass angler.

TACKLE TOOLS

It really doesn't take a lot of tools for maintaining, repairing or even building most fishing tackle. But again, it depends on how deeply you become involved. For instance, rod building is a fun hobby that allows you to create the rod that suits your own style. And, if you really want to get involved, making your own fishing plugs and other lures can become extremely addictive.

Working on fishing tackle, maintaining, cleaning and even building tackle is a fun hobby.

Building fishing rods is a lot of fun, and you can customize a rod to suit your own fishing style. Rod blanks, guides, winding, handles and handle components are all readily available. Most do-it-yourself rod handles are cork, often glued up in segments slipped over the rod butt and then hand shaped. A wood rasp and sandpaper are all that are needed for shaping the handle section. A couple of simple tools can make rod winding easier, faster and better looking. The first tool is a "cradle" to hold the blank while winding on the thread for holding the guides in place. This can simply be a wooden cradle a couple of feet long and made of 1 x 6s. Notches cut in the top hold the rod in place during the winding sequence.

A wooden cradle can be a great help in winding or rewinding rod guides and winding.

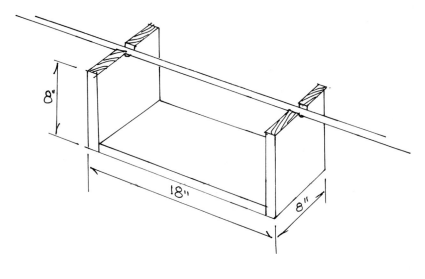

A handmade bobbin also makes it easy to wind on guide thread.

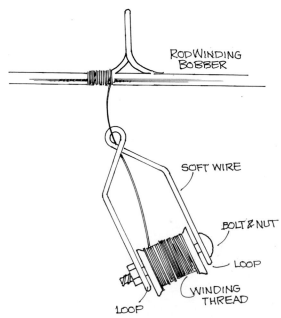

Another handy tool is a homemade "bobbin" to keep the guide-wrapping thread tight while wrapping. The bobbin is made from a piece of heavy wire bent to hold a nut and bolt. The latter holds the wrapping thread spool and is tightened so the spool will just turn with pressure, yet will not unspool when left dangling.

It's also a lot of fun to make your own lures. In addition to pouring simple jigs, with the right tools you can even make your own wooden plugs and spinners. Jigs are the simplest and easiest lures to create and since many, such as crappie lures, are often readily lost, it's economical to pour your own. Molds are available in all sizes and shapes. You'll also need a method of melting the lead. A propane torch and

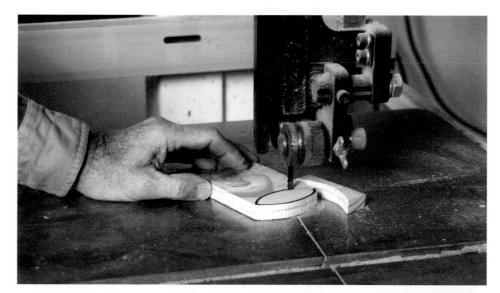

Making your own fishing plugs can be a lot of fun. You'll need woodworking tools.

Making jigs is a very simple chore that allows you to make these popular lures economically. You'll need a means of melting the lead and molds for the jigs.

lead ladle or an electric lead pot can be used for lead melting. Note: You should do this outside to prevent breathing the fumes from the melting lead.

If you want to try your hand at creating your own wooden plugs, it's a bit more complicated and requires more tools. Many plugs are symmetrical and they're best turned on a lathe. Or the plug may have symmetrical parts that are turned on a lathe and then a bandsaw is used to further "rough-shape" the lures. Some plugs are rough shaped entirely on the lathe. A sharp wooden carving knife, wooden rasps and files and a variety of sandpaper can also be used to shape wooden plugs. You'll also need a small drill and bits for drilling holes for hardware and hook attachment screws.

Tying flies is a fun hobby that can add to your fishing enjoyment. Although individual parts and particles are available, full fly-tying kits complete with a vise, hooks, winding thread, feathers and furs are available. The White River Fly-Tying Kits from Bass Pro include a full set of tools and materials plus an instructional video that takes you through each step. The most productive fly patterns are chosen for each type of kit. The kits include trout, bass and jig.

Rods and reels rarely need a lot of maintenance, but occasionally a screw may come loose. Lubrication is an important part of reel maintenance. A set of small screwdrivers, including a jeweler's set, can be mighty handy. Rods may require a bit of regluing or reattaching of rod tips. This is primarily a glue and hold in place job.

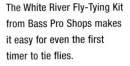

The White River Fly-Tying Kit from Bass Pro Shops makes it easy for even the first timer to tie flies.

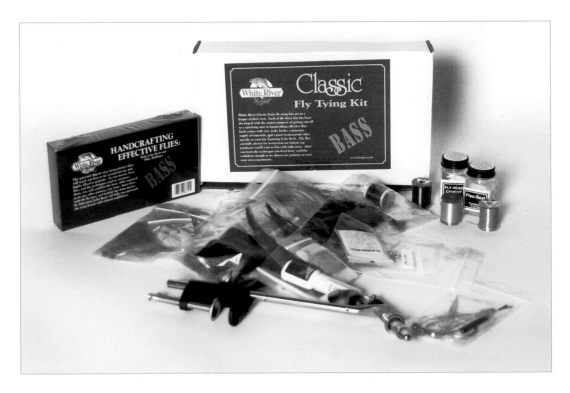

ROD STORAGE

Proper rod storage is extremely important, regardless of the type of species used for. Fishing rods often get stacked in a corner where they become entangled, fall over and sometimes get broken. Leaned together against a garage wall, fishing rods quickly become so entangled you can spend a great deal of your fishing season untangling them. Manufactured rod holders are available from a number of sources. One type I've used for many years, the Berkley Rod Racks, come in five styles and a bottom and top holding rack for holding rods horizontal or vertical. Merely fasten in place to the wall. A friend of mine has also developed a different style of rod rack that can be used to store rods horizontal and overhead in a garage. The stainless steel holders fit in pegboard or slotted boards and hold rods securely in place. These are great for long rods such as surf rods.

You can also make your own rod racks. Following are three different types. The two wall-mounted rod holders shown make rod organization easy. And, they'll look good in your garage or den. The vertical rod holder holds 8 rods and has storage

Rod storage is extremely important in order to keep your rods safe and readily available. I've used the purchased Berkley Rod Racks for years. They're fastened to the wall, or even ceiling.

beneath for fishing line and accessories. The rod holder can sit on the floor, or be attached to a wall. The horizontal rod rack is for storing surf and other long and large rods and reels and is made to be attached to the wall. Simply space the holders the distance needed for your rod lengths. Both of these models were made of No. 2 white pine. They could also be made from hardwoods such as oak or walnut to match furniture or trim. Both models are assembled with self-starting wood screws and glue. Wood plugs to match the wood are cut and placed over the screws to conceal them.

The rotating rod rack is a space saver. It can be stood in a corner or other out-of-the-way place. This rotating rack can hold up to 16 rods without tangling and is similar to the ones you often see in sporting goods store displays.

An unusual rod rack is the stainless steel EZ Rod Organizer shown from S & B Partners. It can be used with pegboard or slotted board to hold rods up and out of the way.

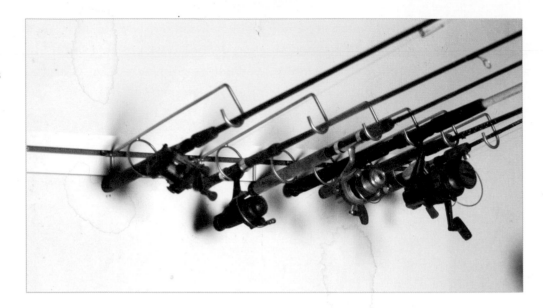

You can also make your own rod racks. The vertical rod rack can be stood against a wall and has space beneath for line.

Vertical Rod Rack

The first step is to enlarge the squared drawing for the side pieces and create a pattern. Trace the pattern off onto the boards and cut the outlines. A band saw or saber saw can be used to make the cuts. The edges should then be well sanded. A drum sander fitted in a drill press makes this chore quick and easy. Locate the position of the screws driven from the sides into the shelves and back strips. Drill the screw holes and then use a larger bit to counterbore the plug holes. Sand both faces of the sides and set them aside. Cut the

bottom shelf board to size and sand it as well. Then cut the bottom rod butt shelf to size. Locate the holes in it for the rod butts. Use a drill press and mortising bits to drill these holes. A backer block should be beneath the work piece to prevent the bit splintering out the back when the bit breaks through the wood.

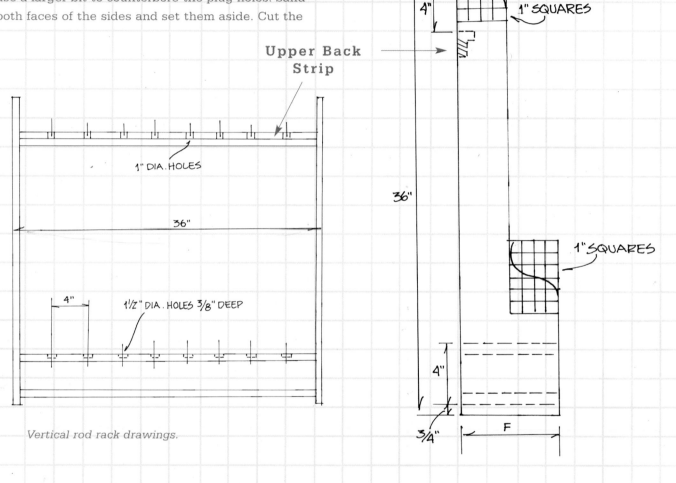

Vertical rod rack drawings.

Materials

Qty.	Part	Dimensions
2	Sides	$3/4$ x 8 x 44"
1	Bottom shelf	$3/4$ x 8 x 48"
1	Bottom rod butt shelf	$3/4$ x 8 x 48"
1	Rod butt support strip	$3/4$ x 2 x 48"
1	Upper rod shelf	$3/4$ x $4^{1}/2$ x 48" (cut to correct width of $3^{1}/2$", after boring holes)
1	Upper back strip	$3/4$ x 2 x 48"

Cut the bottom back strip. Then fasten the bottom rod butt shelf down on top of the bottom back strip with screws up through the bottom edge of the bottom back strip. Cut the rod support strip to size and fasten it in place on the underside of the bottom rod butt shelf. Cut a piece of stock to the correct length for the upper rod shelf. It should be 1" wider than the finished piece. Mark the locations of the rod-holding "slots" and bore holes with the forstner bit and drill press to create the slots. Then rip 1" off the front of the board. This creates the notches quickly and easily. Sand the cut front edge smooth. Cut the top shelf back board to width and length. Fasten the upper rod shelf down on the top shelf back board. Use screws driven from the bottom edge of the back board up into the upper rod shelf.

Now you're ready to assemble the sides to the rod-holding shelves. Using the predrilled and counter-bored holes, fasten the shelves to one side with self-starting wood screws. Then stand the shelf on the end and fasten the opposite side in place. Wood-worker's glue can also be used to further strengthen the assembly. Then cut the wood plugs to cover the screws. Apply a bit of glue on each plug and tap in place. When all glue has set, sand and finish the rack. To install on the wall, drive screws through the upper and lower back strips into wall studs.

Horizontal Rod Rack

Cut the back strips and rod support strips to length and round their corners using a saber saw or band-saw. Smooth up the rounded corners using a drum sander in a drill press. Locate the positions for the holes in the rod support strips and mark. Bore the rod support holes using a forstner bit in a drill press. Use a backer board to assure the bit doesn't splinter out the holes when it comes through the stock. Use a saber saw to cut the slots in to meet the bored holes. Bore and countersink for the screws in the back of the back strips. Sand all pieces well and then fasten the rod support strips to the back strips with self-starting screws through the back strips and into the edges of the rod support strips. Finish to suit.

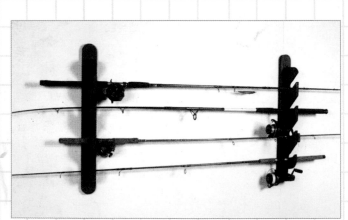

Horizontal rod rack consists of two racks, fastened to a wall. The racks can be spaced the length needed for the rods, providing storage space for long rods.

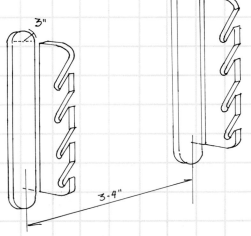

Horizontal rod rack drawing.

Materials

Qty.	Part	Dimensions
2	Back strips	¾ x 3 x 30"
2	Rod support strips	¾ x 4½ x 24"

Rotating Rod Rack

A standing rotating rod rack can be made fairly easily and can stand in a corner for out-of-the-way storage of 16 rods. The stand consists of three disks held with a center support rod. The disks should be made of plywood or a good solid hardwood, such as oak. First step is to lay out the disks on the plywood using a compass. Then divide the circles into 16 segments as shown in the drawing using a straight edge. Mark the locations for the rod butt indentations in the bottom holding piece. Also mark the exact center of the circle. Cut the bottom support circle using a band saw or saber saw and then sand the edge smooth. Using a forstner bit, cut the rod butt indentations in the support circle. Note, these are only $3/8$" deep. This is best done on a drill press, so the exact depth of the holes can be set. You can use a portable electric drill to drill the holes if you use a piece of masking tape on the drill bit to create a depth "gauge." The bottom base piece is cut on a band saw and the edge sanded as well.

The top holding disk should be laid out with the holes marked on the disk, but don't cut the disk out yet. Instead, bore the holes through for the rod holders, then cut the disk out and sand all edges smooth. Note the holes are bored on the edge so there is just a slight opening in the edge for the rod tip to slip in place.

The center support can be constructed in one of two manners. A $1\frac{1}{2}$" wooden dowel can be used, or you can turn the support piece on a lathe. In the latter case, a wooden "cap" is also turned to finish off the piece. To create the turning, enlarge the squared drawing and make a pattern for the turning.

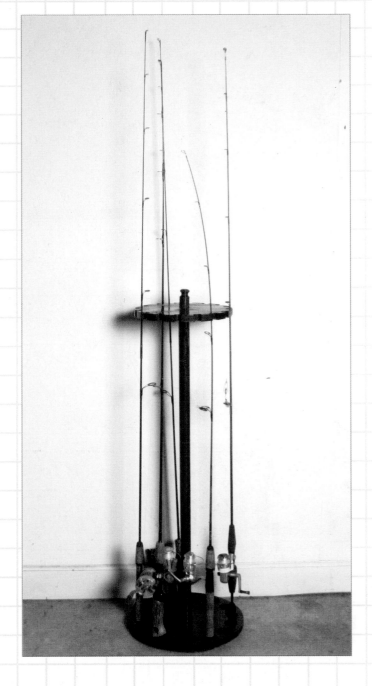

Rotating rod rack is a space saver. It can be stood in a corner and rotated to retrieve rods desired.

Materials

Qty.	Part	Dimensions
1	Bottom disk, $3/4$" plywood	12 x 12"
1	Bottom support disk, $3/4$" plywood	14 x 14"
1	Top support disk, $3/4$" plywood	8 x 8"
1	Support spindle	2 x 2 x 36"
1	Top decorative spindle	2 x 2 x 2"
	Screws, washer or turntable	
	Felt, scrap pieces	

Rotating Rod Rack cont'd

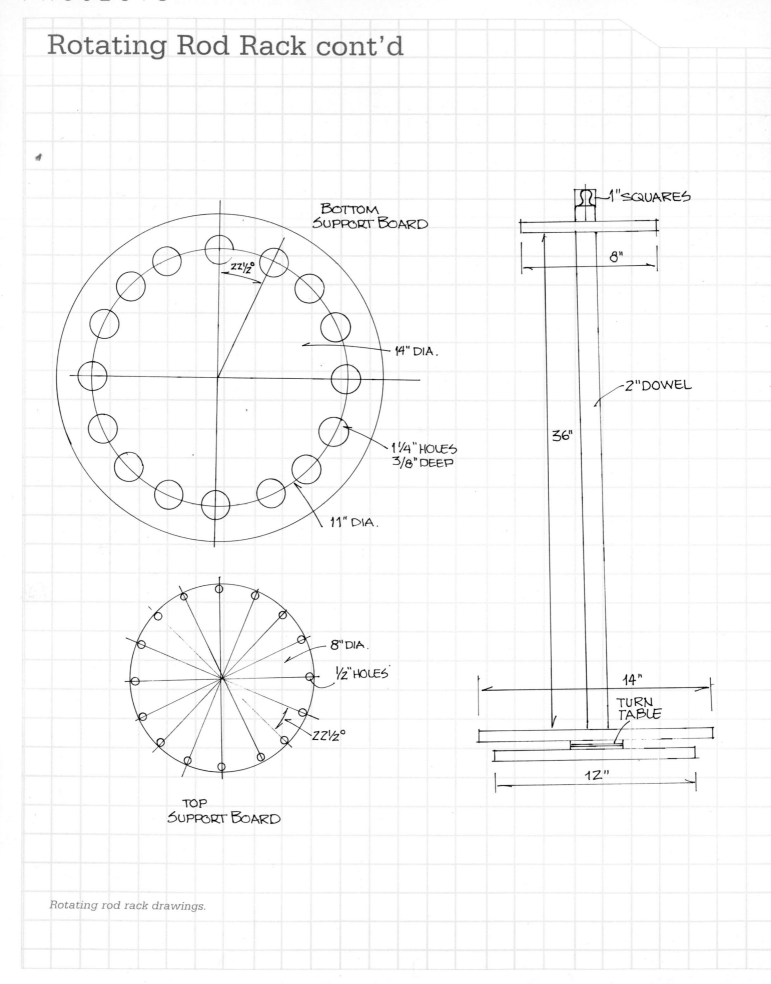

BOTTOM
SUPPORT BOARD

22½°

14" DIA.

1¼" HOLES
3/8" DEEP

11" DIA.

8" DIA.

½" HOLES

22½°

TOP
SUPPORT BOARD

1" SQUARES

8"

2" DOWEL

36"

14"

TURN
TABLE

12"

Rotating rod rack drawings.

First step in construction is to lay out the circles and mark the locations of the holes.

Bore the $^3/_8$" deep holes in the bottom circle after it has been cut out.

Bore the holes in the smaller top piece with a forstner bit in a drill press, before you cut out the top circle.

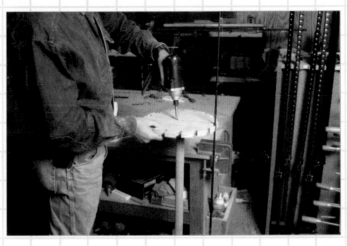

Assemble the bottom and top circles to the support rod with glue and screws.

Assemble the unit by first fastening the bottom support piece to the center support piece with glue and screws, keeping the screws off center. Then fasten the bottom piece under the bottom support piece with a large screw, using a large washer as a "bearing." Or-you can utilize a small lazy-susan turntable, such as that from Rockler, for easier turning of the rod holder base. If using a turntable, fasten it to the bottom disk, then turn the lower portion of the turntable at right angles. Bore $^1/_2$" diameter holes at these locations. This provides an opening to install the turntable on the bottom support piece.

Fasten the upper support disk to the top of the support spindle, again with screws and glue, but keeping the screws away from the center of the disk. To make sure the holes align with the rod butt holes, position a couple of rods temporarily in place. Then add the top spindle piece, using a wooden dowel through the bottom of the top spindle piece and into the top disk.

Provide a stain and finish coat as desired. Then add felt to the inside of the top disk rod support holes.

Rod Transporting Case

Another form of rod storage involves safely protecting rods during transport, whether on planes, automobiles or even at-home storage. In one overseas airline flight my very solid purchased rod case came out of the conveyor almost bent into a U shape. I knew then the trip wasn't going to be good.

You can, however, build a very solid rod case. And it's simple. All you need is a section of PVC plumbing pipe. The diameter of the pipe is determined by the amount and size of rods you intend to transport. You will also need a couple of end caps of the appropriate size. Cut the pipe to the correct length using a hacksaw. Then carefully sand all cut edges extremely smooth. Plastic pipe can cut, so you might wish to wear leather gloves. Using PVC glue, glue one end cap in place. Sand the inside of the second cap so it will slide on and off the end of the PVC pipe easily. If you want a non-secure transport, simply use a pair of eye-hooks and a bungee cord to make sure the end cap stays in place. For more secure transport, attach a small padlock hasp to the end cap and pipe. You will have to bend the hasp pieces to fit, but it's not really a problem if you have a solid vise. Then attach a screen-door handle as a carry handle. Cut two pieces of foam and add one to each end to protect rod tips and butts.

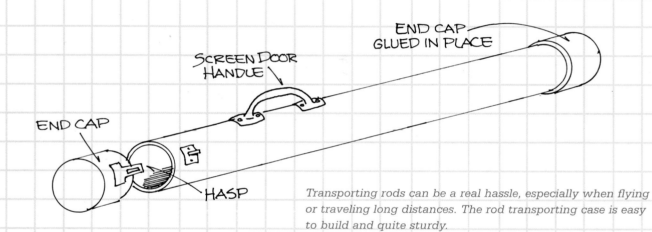

END CAP GLUED IN PLACE

SCREEN DOOR HANDLE

END CAP

HASP

Transporting rods can be a real hassle, especially when flying or traveling long distances. The rod transporting case is easy to build and quite sturdy.

Materials

Qty.	Part
1	Length of PVC pipe
2	End caps
1	Screen door handle
1	Hasp

TACKLE STORAGE

Tackle storage can include everything from lures and baits to rainsuits and we've included storage solutions for all. We've also included a tackle bench to use as a work station for everything from tying flies to replacing the line on your favorite reel.

Tackle storage can run the gamut from a locker full of bass plugs to a handful of flies.

Fly-Tying Chest

Wooden chests were very popular in the past to hold valuable lures, and especially fly-tying materials. Traditionally the chests are made of oak, and with felt-lined or padded drawers for holding delicate materials. You can easily make your own "traditional-style" chest to hold your fly-tying materials and a vise.

The fly-tying chest shown not only has space for tying materials, but safe storage for your best flies as well.

The chest shown is made entirely of red oak. It is fastened together with countersunk wood screws covered with red-oak wood plugs that are sanded flush with the wood surfaces. First step is to secure stock wide enough for the top, bottom, back, inside shelf and sides. You may have to glue up the stock if you can't find wide stock. Although the chest shown has a lift-up lid, the box is assembled first, and then the upper-lid portion cut from the box with a table saw. Cut the sides to the correct size. Then cut tiny wood

Materials

Qty.	Part	Dimensions
1	Top	$1/2$ x $9^1/2$ x 24"
2	Ends	$1/2$ x $9^1/2$ x 12"
1	Bottom	$1/2$ x 9 x 23"
1	Back	$1/2$ x 12 x 23"
1	Top front	$1/2$ x $3^3/4$ x 23"
1	Top open section, bottom	$1/4$ x 9 x 23"
1	Open section bottom support cleats	$1/2$ x $1/2$ x 60" cut to fit
2	Middle drawers, fronts	$1/2$ x $1^7/8$ x 23"
1	Bottom drawer, front	$1/2$ x $3^1/8$ x 23"
6	Drawer slides	$1/2$ x $3/8$ x 8"
4	Middle drawers, sides	$1/2$ x $1^7/8$ x 8"
2	Middle drawers, backs	$1/2$ x $1^7/8$ x 23"
3	Drawer bottoms	$1/2$ x $7^1/2$ x $22^1/2$"
2	Bottom drawer, sides	$1/2$ x $3^1/8$ x 8"
1	Bottom drawer, back	$1/2$ x $3^1/8$ x 23"
8	Brass corners	
1 pr.	Brass hinges	
6	Brass knobs	
2	Brass top latches	
2	Brass side handles	
	Felt or flocking	

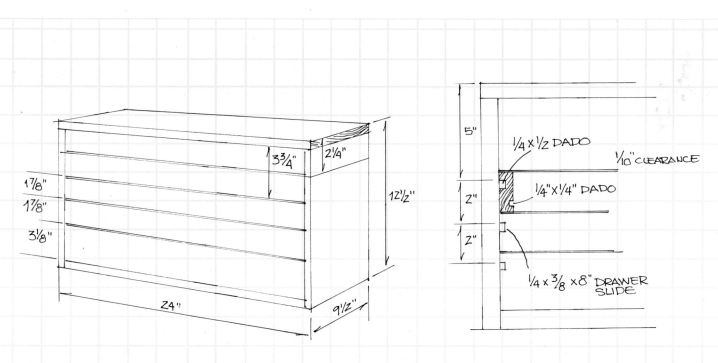

Fly-tying chest drawings.

drawer slides and glue and fasten them in place on the inside of the sides. To assure the slides are square, mark their locations with a small woodworking square. Join the front piece to both sides with wood screws countersunk from the front piece into the sides. Cut the back and fasten it in place with screws in from the two sides. Then cut the bottom and fasten it in place. Cut the inside shelf piece and fasten in place. Note it fits down on cleats fastened to the inside of the back, sides and front piece. These are fastened with glue and screws from the inside of the case. Cut the top to correct size and fasten it down over the sides, back and front piece, again with countersunk wood screws.

Set the table saw to a 2¼" wide cut, remove the splitter and saw guard and carefully cut around the assembled box, with the top against the saw fence. This separates the top lid from the bottom of the chest. The Freud Glue-Line Ripping blade makes an extremely fine cut that allows the cut edges to join together smoothly.

The drawer front and sides have ¼" dadoes cut on their inside edges to hold ¼" hardboard bottom boards. The sides must also have a dado cut to allow them to slide on the tiny wood drawer slides. Make all these cuts with a router, or a table saw with the kicker and guard removed and either a dado head or simply making progressive cuts with a regular blade to create the dado width needed. The back is cut to the width to allow the bottom board to slide in place. The drawer fronts have rabbets cut on their ends to overlap the drawer sides. These can be cut with a dado head in a table or radial-arm saw.

Assemble the drawers by cutting the drawer sides and backs to the correct sizes. Fasten the sides to the backs with glue and small nails. An air-nailer with brads works great for this. Cut each bottom to the correct size, and then slide it into the dadoes in the sides and back. Place glue on the front dadoes and fit the fronts in place, with the bottoms in the front dado. Use a small woodworker's square to make sure the drawers are square, then clamp securely. Carefully fit the drawers in place. You will probably have to do some hand jointing or sanding to make sure they fit properly.

Finish the inside and outside of the entire case with several coats of polyurethane. You may also wish to line the drawers and top section with felt glued in place. An easier method is to use Suede Tex and the Mini-Flocker that sprays a soft interior liner in place. The products are available from Rockler.

The chest is finished off with brass knobs, brass corners, brass hasps and hinges and handles, all available from Rockler.

Tackle Storage Cabinet

Proper tackle storage is extremely important. A cabinet to hold fishing rods, tackle boxes, jackets, nets and other gear can keep the clutter off your garage floor and protect your valuable investment. The cabinet shown is over 6' inside in order to accommodate 6' rods. You may prefer a shorter or taller cabinet, and it can be changed quit easily. The cabinet is divided into two parts; one side has a clothing rack to hold jackets, and a shelf on top for off-season storage. The other side has shelves to hold tackle boxes, and rods are held in place in rod racks on the door. Since I fish for a number of species, including bass, walleye, crappie, catfish, striper and occasionally saltwater species, I've devised a tackle storage system for my cabinet utilizing individual Plano plastic tackle boxes. Lures are sorted according to species or category and stored in separate boxes, for instance bass topwaters, bass mid-depth runners, bass deep runners, plastic worms, plastic lizards and so forth. The same system also works for my other favorite species. At a glance, I can pull out what I need for the day's fishing. For instance, bass fishing early in the spring I know I don't need a lot of topwater lures, so out comes the pig and jig boxes and spinnerbaits. If I'm fishing early-season walleye, out comes suspending jerkbaits.

The cabinet shown is made of ³⁄₄" plywood, and can be good-one-side (B-C) fir, birch or even oak if you prefer a nicer finished cabinet. The interior divider and shelves are also of plywood. The back is of ¹⁄₄" plywood. Hardboard could be substituted for the back if you prefer.

If you fish for a lot of species, as I do, you'll need lots of organized storage. Small individual boxes, labeled as to contents, allows you to take what you need for the day and keep the rest safely stored.

Materials

Qty.	Part	Dimensions
2	Sides, ³⁄₄" plywood	24 x 80"
1	Top, ³⁄₄" plywood	24 x 46"
1	Bottom ³⁄₄" plywood	23¹⁄₄ x 46¹⁄₂"
1	Back, ¹⁄₄" plywood	48 x 80"
1	Bottom kick board, ³⁄₄" plywood	2 x 46¹⁄₂"
1	Inside vertical divider, ³⁄₄" plywood	24 x 76¹⁄₂"
4	Shelf support strips	³⁄₄ x 1¹⁄₂ x 16", cut to fit
2	Top shelves, ³⁄₄" plywood	16 x 22¹⁄₂", cut to fit
	Adjustable shelves, ³⁄₄" plywood	16 x 21¹⁄₂", cut to fit
2	Doors, ³⁄₄" plywood	24 x 79"
	Closet pole and brackets	
	Adjustable shelf support strips and brackets	
	Hinges, door handles	
	Magnetic catches	

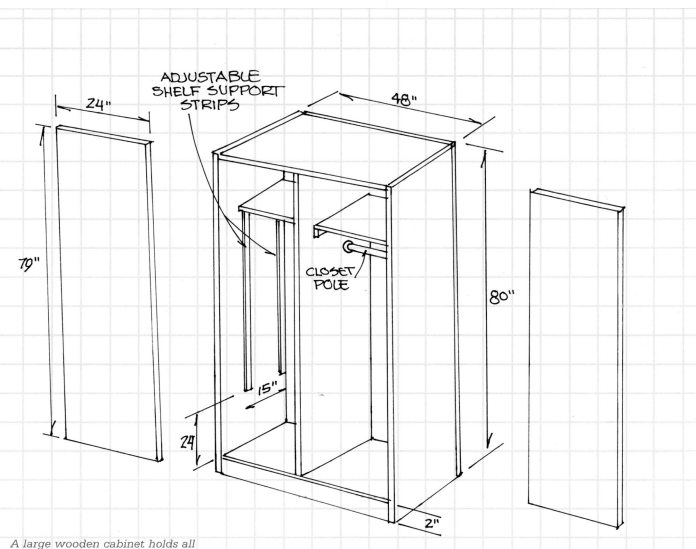

ADJUSTABLE
SHELF SUPPORT
STRIPS

24"

48"

79"

CLOSET
POLE

80"

15"

24

2"

*A large wooden cabinet holds all
the individual boxes.*

First step in construction is to cut the sides, top and bottom pieces to the correct length and width. My favorite tactic for cutting large sheets of plywood is to place the plywood across a couple of sawhorses. Then set a circular saw blade to cut just through the plywood, but just barely into the sawhorses. Measure and snap a chalk line or use a straight edge to create the cut line. Cut the pieces to size. Fasten one side to the top and bottom pieces using glue and self-starting wood screws. Note the bottom piece is set up 2" from the bottom edges of the side pieces. Fasten the opposite side in place in the same manner. Then cut the center divider and fasten it between the top and bottom pieces. Cut the back and lay it in place over the assembled cabinet back. Note the back runs to the bottom edges of the sides. Use a carpenter's square to assure the cabinet is square, and then fasten the back in place.

Cut the shelf support strips and fasten them in place. Then cut the shelves and install them down on the support strips. Adjustable shelves can be added in one side by adding shelf cleats and clips to the open side of the cabinet. Cut and install the closet pole. Note there is a bottom "kick" board reaching from the floor to the top of the bottom. Cut this and install it in place. Then cut the two doors to size and hinge them in place. Add a lock, or magnetic catches and knobs to the doors.

Tackle Bench

Although a fishing tackle work-bench doesn't have to be as solid, nor as complicated, as a gun-smithing bench, it still needs to be sturdy and have storage for tools and supplies.

   The bench shown is quite simple to build, and can easily fit against a garage wall and leave plenty of room for your vehicle. The bench is constructed of standard 2 x 4s and features a smooth flat top for holding small items. A shelf on the bottom and drawers add to the storage space. It's important to match the height of the bench to your stature or working technique. The bench shown is 36" for easy stand-up working or for use with a stool. Using self-starting wood screws makes assembly of the bench quick and easy.

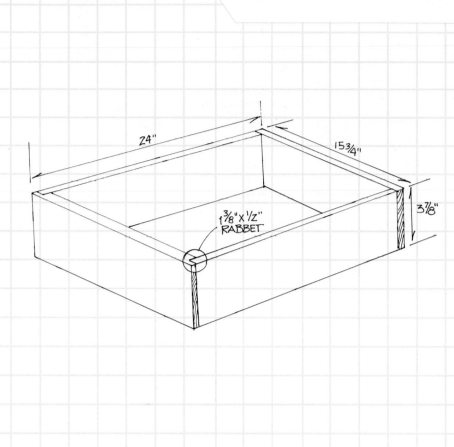

You'll need a work table or bench. The bench shown has a shelf beneath for storage, as well as three drawers for additional storage.

Materials

Qty.	Part	Dimensions
4	Legs	2 x 4 x 35$\frac{1}{4}$"
2	Top back and front supports	2 x 4 x 57"
1	Back bottom support	2 x 4 x 57"
2	Top side supports	2 x 4 x 30"
1	Top, $\frac{3}{4}$" plywood	30 x 60"
2	Bottom side supports	2 x 4 x 28$\frac{1}{2}$"
1	Bottom shelf, $\frac{3}{4}$" plywood	18 x 60"
2	Sides	$\frac{3}{4}$ x 8 x 27"
2	Front horizontal facers	$\frac{3}{4}$ x 2 x 56"
4	Vertical facers	$\frac{3}{4}$ x 2 x 4"
6	Drawer sides	$\frac{1}{2}$ x 3$\frac{7}{8}$ x 24", cut to fit
3	Drawer fronts	$\frac{3}{4}$ x 3$\frac{7}{8}$ x 15$\frac{3}{4}$"
3	Drawer backs	$\frac{1}{2}$ x 3$\frac{7}{8}$ x 15$\frac{3}{4}$"
3	Drawer bottoms	$\frac{1}{4}$ x 15$\frac{1}{4}$ x 23$\frac{1}{2}$
3	Drawer knobs	
3 pr.	Drawer slides	

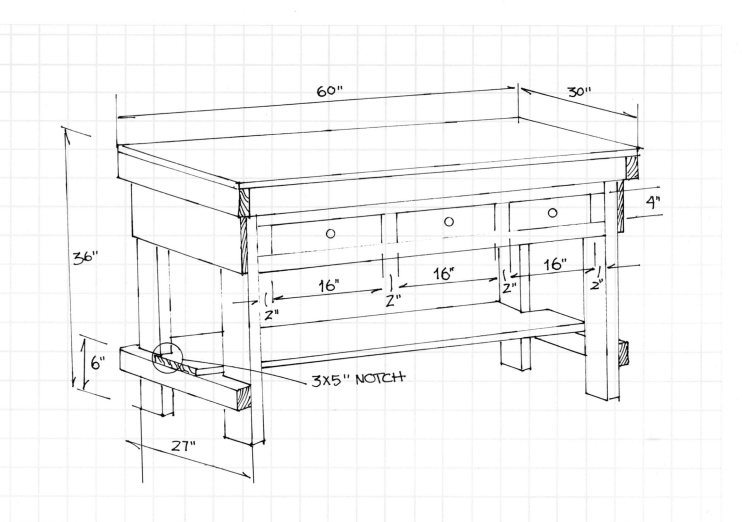

First step in construction is to measure and cut all legs and support pieces to the proper length, making sure the cuts are square. Lay two legs on a smooth, flat surface and position the top rear support piece across them. Drive one screw in each end of the support piece. Then use a carpenter's square to make sure the assembly is square. Drive two more screws in each end of the top support piece. Fasten the bottom rear support piece in place in the same manner. Turn the assembly over with the support boards facing down, and fasten the upper and lower side support boards in place on each end in the same manner with three screws in each end and making sure the assembly is square. Note the top support boards must extend 1½" past the edge of the 2 x 4 in order to fasten the front support board in place. Fasten the top front support board to the legs and then fasten the top end support boards to the top front support.

Notch the plywood shelf to fit around the back legs. Then anchor it in place down on the rear and side bottom support boards with No. 8 x 1½" screws. Make sure the assembly is square.

Cut the front drawer support board and anchor it in place with screws driven through the front legs and into the ends of the support board. Cut the rear drawer support board and install in the same manner. Then cut the horizontal drawer dividers and fasten between the bottom drawer support board and the top front support board. Cut the drawer pieces to the correct size and fasten the drawer together. Commercial drawer slides are quick and easy to use, or you can create your own drawer slides.

Cut the plywood top to the correct size and fasten in place with No. 8 x 1½" screws. These screws should be slightly countersunk to provide a smooth surface. Paint or varnish the bench to provide a protective coating.

BAIT STORAGE

Keeping bait such as minnows, nightcrawlers, crawfish and earthworms is a basic for many anglers. With the right storage equipment, keeping your own bait, even in bulk, is fairly easy.

The biggest problem with worms is when you want them you have to dig in your backyard, or buy high-priced but tiny containers at a bait shop. You can, however, grow your own—and it's fun and easy.

Worms can be purchased through mail order. English red wigglers, called red worms, are a common choice. They are active, a highly prolific variety and are resistant to many misfortunes that can befall other types of worms when grown in captivity. A full grown adult is about 3" long and just a bit over $^1/_8$" in diameter. You can also raise nightcrawlers, but it takes a great deal more expertise and work.

You'll need a box to hold the worms, and a number of excellent worm growing or holding boxes are available from Magic Worm Products. The Magic Worm Ranch is a polystyrene container that is ventilated and insulated. It comes with $4^1/_2$ pounds of bedding and 12 ounces of worm food as well as complete instructions. It's a complete storage unit that will keep hundreds of worms fresh and active.

Keeping bait such as earthworms and crawdads is fairly easy.

Wooden Worm Box

You can also build your own wooden worm box. The box must have air holes to allow for ventilation, yet not allow the worms to crawl out. It must also have a lid that won't allow the worms to crawl out. Because the wood will be in constant contact with damp soil, it must be extremely water resistant. This includes Western white cedar or treated lumber. Shown is an easy-to-make worm box.

The first step is to cut the sides and ends to the right dimensions. Rip the pieces from 1 x 12 stock to the 9" width needed and then cut to the proper lengths. Attach the ends on the sides using self-starting wood screws.

Cut the bottom from $^3/_4$" stock, making sure it is square, and then fasten to the sides and end with self-starting wood screws. Cut the lid sides and ends to dimension from the previously ripped $2^1/_2$" stock. Fasten the lid sides to the ends using self-starting wood screws. Cut the lid top, making sure it is square, and fasten down on the lid sides and ends with self-starting wood screws. Cut the ventilation holes in the top with a hole saw in a portable electric drill, and then fasten screenwire over the inside with staples and a staple gun.

You can even make your own worm farm.

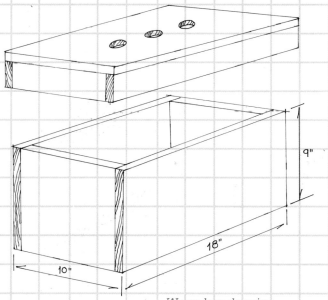

Worm box drawing.

Materials

Qty.	Part	Dimensions
2	Sides	$^3/_4$ x 9 x 18"
2	Ends	$^3/_4$ x 9 x $8^1/_2$"
1	Bottom	$^3/_4$ x $8^1/_2$ x $16^1/_2$"
2	Top, lid sides	$^3/_4$ x $2^1/_2$ x 19"
2	Top, lid ends	$^3/_4$ x $2^1/_2$ x 10"
1	Top	$^3/_4$ x $11^1/_2$ x $19^3/_4$"
1	Screenwire	6 x 8"

Growing Earthworms

Once the container is constructed, fill with good garden soil that is not sandy. Thoroughly mix one cup of dry dog food and then sprinkle about a quart of water over the soil. Place 25 to 50 worms on top of the soil. Dampen a couple of sheets of newsprint and place over the worms.

Place the worm farm in a cool part of your basement, away from the furnace, but where the temperature will stay around 60°F. Temperature is very important. If the temperature rises much above 70°F, the worms may die; if the temperature drops below 60°F, reproduction may be slowed.

Inspect your worm farm once a week. If the surface is dry, add a little water, but don't overwater. If the soil is muddy or moldy, you're overfeeding and/or overwatering. About every three weeks remove the top 2–3" of soil and mix in one-half cup of dry dog food. Dump the remainder of the soil out and check your worm "herd." Place the newly fed soil on the bottom of the container and replace the rest of the soil and the worms. In six to eight weeks you should have a new crop of worms. And, if you're a good worm farmer, you can expect anywhere from 700 to 1,000 worms.

Raising nightcrawlers, on the other hand, is a bit tricky. But you can keep a large supply for use over a long period of time if you have a refrigerator and a worm box that fits inside it. Just don't allow the worms to freeze.

Minnow Tank

One of the biggest frustrations of crappie angling, especially during the hot weather months, is keeping minnows alive and frisky. It's a problem on the water, and if you have minnows left over from a trip and want to keep them for a few days, or until the next weekend, it's even tougher. Or, if you're like me and want to get on the water before daylight, you'll often find marinas or bait dealers not open, or perhaps you live where there just aren't any minnow dealers or bait shops. Perhaps you're a catfishing addict and keeping large numbers of goldfish, big minnows and crawfish alive is a problem. A wide range of aerated bait buckets can keep your bait alive longer and friskier while on the water, and also for short periods of time between trips. Marine Metal Products has several models, including their Super Bait Saver Tanks ranging 5–20 gallons. Frabil Aqua-Life Bait Stations also come in several sizes and feature micro-bubble oxygen aerators. The Bait Tamer and Commercial Bait Storage Containers from Lindy-Little Joe are also great choices.

Or you can do as I did and make up your own. Several years ago when I wanted an even larger tank for keeping minnows for crappie and walleye fishing, I created a tank system as good as in many bait shops from a handful of supplies. I utilized a Rubbermaid 50-gallon polyethylene stock tank for the tank portion, placing it in a

Keeping minnows is fairly easy with a wide number of today's aerated minnow buckets.

shady spot under my garden shed overhang. This tank has a drain plug in the bottom, and I fitted a section of garden hose to the drain with a shut-off so I could occasionally drain off a bit of water and run in fresh. A commercial 110-volt aerator provides aeration. A wooden lid prevents minnows from jumping out. A floating foam block provides a place for crawfish to crawl out on.

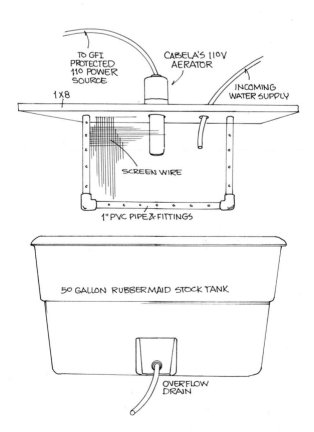

You can also make up a "bulk" minnow-keeping tank with a stock tank and 110-volt aerator.

Floating Bait and Live Box

If you have a pond or small lake, or own a dock on a lake, this combined bait box and live box will be extremely handy. One side can be used to keep a supply of minnow or crawfish readily at hand, while the opposite side can be used to keep fish alive until you find it convenient to dress them. Most states have rules governing the keeping of live game fish, so you should check with the local conservation authorities concerning the ruling in your particular state or area.

We use the live box in our pond primarily as a holding box for fish. Quite often one member of the family may wander down to the pond for a few moments of relaxation, not a full-fledged fishing trip. The result is usually one or two fish, or a handful of bluegill. They are simply plunked into the holding box until we get enough fish collected for a fish fry. The opposite side holds a good supply of min-

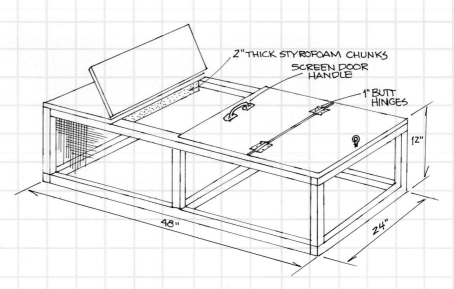

A floating combination bait and live box can keep bait alive at a pond and also act as a live well for holding fish.

nows or crawfish. When we get ready for a trotlining trip to the river, we spend a day seining minnows and crawfish and keep them in the bait box lively and healthy until we're ready for the trip.

The box is quite simple to make and if you wish a smaller, single-sided unit it would be quite easy to simply halve the size of the box. The box is simply a framework of 2 x 2s. These can be purchased at any lumber or building supply yard, or you can simply buy 2 x 4s and rip them to the correct size. Fasten together with brass or other weather-resistant screws. Then cover the inside divider, bottom and all the outside with window screening or small-mesh hardware cloth, stapling it solidly in place to the 2 x 2s. Cut a

1 x 12 to the correct length and fasten to each outer end with screws. Then screw an eye bolt in each end for tying the floating box to a dock. Cut the 1 x 12 doors to size and hinge them to the end top pieces. Fasten a screen door handle on each door top. Doors can also be scraps of marine-grade plywood if you have them on hand.

Plastic foam chunks 2" thick are installed up under the outer ends of the box as flotation. Now all that's left is to fill the box with bait and fish.

Materials

Qty.	Part	Dimensions
4	Top and bottom side pieces	$1\frac{1}{2}$ x $1\frac{1}{2}$ x 45"
6	Vertical pieces	$1\frac{1}{2}$ x $1\frac{1}{2}$ x 9"
6	Horizontal pieces	$1\frac{1}{2}$ x $1\frac{1}{2}$ x 24"
2	Top ends	$\frac{3}{4}$ x 12 x 24"
2	Doors	$\frac{3}{4}$ x 12 x 24"
2	Hinges	
2	Pulls	
2	Eye hooks	
	Screenwire and staples	24" x 48"
	Styrofoam chunks for flotation	

Bait Trap

The trap shown is simply made of $^1/_4$ x $^1/_4$" galvanized wire (netting). The first step is to lay out and cut the bottom and top circular pieces. Cut a hole in the top piece. Make sure you understand the size of hole that is allowed for bait traps (see note). Then cut the outside piece to size. Wire the entire assembly together with light-gauge wire. Add 6-ounce sinkers to the bottom edge, again wiring in place. Attach the cord and to the top add a bottle float as a marker. Note: Before making and using a bait trap make sure you read and understand the laws in your state or province regarding the use of bait traps, such as what is considered bait, size of entrance opening and so forth.

To use, crumble up bread and drop in the bait trap. Make up a doughball mixture of flour and water and press around the outside edge of the opening. The mixture should be fairly stiff. This will continually melt, creating an attractant that will attract baitfish. Place in a shallow water location next to weeds, wood structure or other areas that baitfish inhabit and leave for a few hours. Again make sure you understand bait-catching rules for your area. You have to check bait traps on a regular basis.

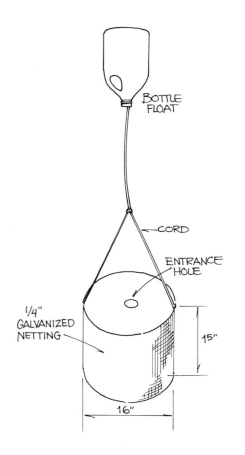

You can make up your own minnow trap fairly easily.

CHAPTER 3

Hunting and Shooting Sports Equipment Storage

Storage of hunting gear and clothing can vary a great deal, depending on the type of hunting you do. For instance, upland and waterfowling gear have different requirements, as does deer hunting and small game. Although some hunters will specialize in one sport, if you're like me, you like to hunt them all and that takes a lot of storage and organizing. Of course, there's also the dog gear and storage. In addition to hunting, shooting sports also have their own gear and requirements. Following are suggestions on storage for the various sports, as well as the tools needed to maintain and repair the various pieces of gear.

An alternative to cabinets, shelves and racks is a lockable, walk-in storage room or closet. If storing guns and other valuables, you will probably want to use a steel door with a lock and deadbolt. It won't prevent dedicated thieves from breaking in, but may slow them down and/or discourage them.

WATERFOWLING GEAR STORAGE

Waterfowling means just what it says, water and quite often mud. And there's a lot of gear involved in this sport. Clothing, boots, calls, decoys, blinds, boats, gear bags, guns and miscellany are often wet and muddy at the end of the day. Proper storage is important not only to maintain peace in the household, but also to allow your gear proper drying in order to preserve it. The first step, if you can afford it, is to have a mud-room where you can store the muddy clothes and gear. Or, fix an area in your garage for the purpose. Once the muddy gear dries, you can knock off the big chunks and sweep or vacuum up the dried mud and dirt.

Hanging Boot Rack

One of the biggest frustrations of waterfowling is leaky waders, and one of the most common causes of leaks is tossing boots in a corner and allowing them to be stored folded down. For longevity, and to allow the boots to dry, the best tactic is to store them hanging upside down. A simple plywood rack can be constructed to hold boots in that manner. Enlarge the squared drawing and make a pattern for the boot holding shelf. Then cut it to shape using a saber saw or band saw. Round and smooth all edges. Cut the back and the side supports from plywood. Fasten the pieces together with glue and screws. Attach the rack to a wall. If possible anchor it to a stud because waterfowling waders can be fairly heavy.

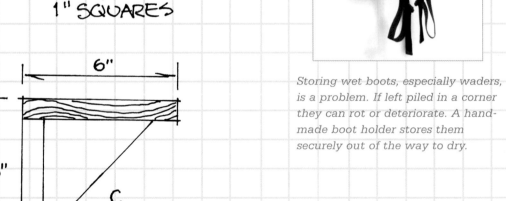

Storing wet boots, especially waders, is a problem. If left piled in a corner they can rot or deteriorate. A handmade boot holder stores them securely out of the way to dry.

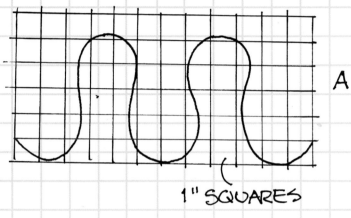

A

1" SQUARES

6"

6"

C

B

Boot rack drawings.

Materials

	Qty.	Part	Dimensions
A	1	Boot shelf, $3/4$" plywood	6 x 12"
B	1	Back support piece, $3/4$" plywood	6 x 12"
C	1	Shelf support, $3/4$" plywood	$4^1/2$ x $4^1/2$"

Waterfowling Rack

Combining boot holders with a clothing rack and gear shelf provides an all-in-one place for waterfowl gear storage. The rack shown has room for three boots, and plenty of clothing hanging area. The shelf above can hold gear bags and other items. And, since it's fairly high and out of reach, the shelf could even be used to store ammo. Space below the shelf, clothing and boots can be used to store decoys. The boot holding shelves are made of $3/4$" plywood, while the remaining parts of the rack are made of standard 1 x 12, soft pine materials, readily available as shelving lumber at home suppliers.

Waterfowling storage rack holds boots up off the floor and open to dry, with a shelf for calls, ammunition and other gear.

Materials

Qty.	Part	Dimensions
3	Boot shelves, $3/4$" plywood	6 x 12"
3	Boot shelf supports, $3/4$" plywood	$4^1/2$ x $4^1/2$"
1	Boot shelf horizontal support	$3/4$ x 4 x $70^1/2$"
2	Ends, $3/4$" plywood	$11^1/2$ x 14"
1	Top shelf	$3/4$ x $11^1/2$ x 72"
1	Top shelf support	$3/4$ x 4 x $70^1/2$"
	Coat hanger hooks, to suit	

Waterfowling Rack cont'd

First step is to enlarge the squared drawing and make a pattern for the boot holding shelves. Cut to shape using a band saw or saber saw, and then sand all edges smooth. Cut the horizontal back shelf support. Rip this from a 1 x 12 using a circular saw or table or radial arm saw. Fasten the boot shelf in place to the horizontal support and add the shelf supports. Use glue and screws to fasten together.

Cut the ends to size and shape. Note their front edges are angled. Cut these using a saber saw, or portable circular saw. Cut the top shelf to length. Then fasten the top shelf down on the top edges of the ends using glue and screws. Position the assem- bled boot/clothing shelf in place and fasten with glue and screws as well. Rip the top shelf brace to size and cut to length. Fasten it between the ends and up under the top shelf with glue and screws.

Sand all portions of the rack smooth. The rack can be left as is, although a coat of finish will provide protection. You can also stain and finish. Because of all the mud involved, I simply painted the rack shown with exterior brown paint. The next step is to anchor the rack/shelf to the wall, and you'll need help to hold it in place. Make sure the shelf is anchored well with screws into the studs.

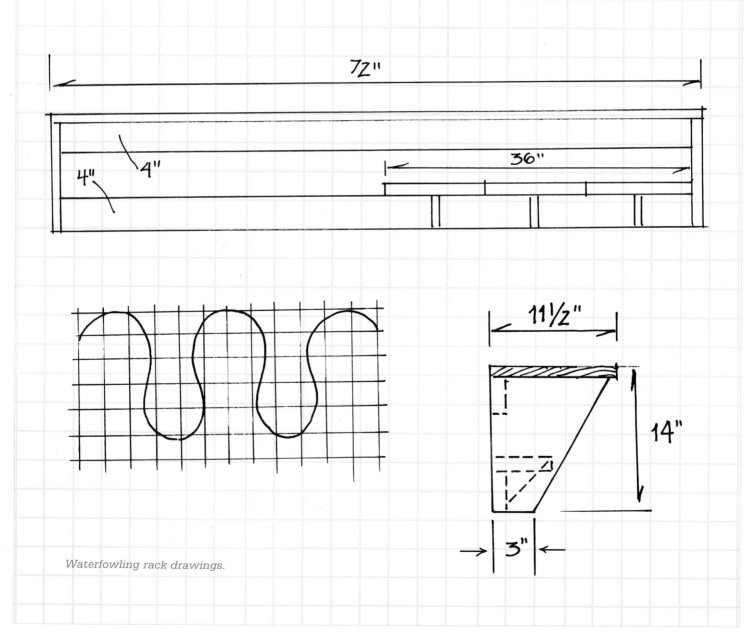

Waterfowling rack drawings.

Decoy Storage

Decoy storage is one of the biggest problems with many waterfowlers, especially serious goose hunters with hundreds of goose decoys. Our day-to-day storage of duck decoys and a dozen goose decoys for small water hunting is under the waterfowling rack shown, left in the truck bed for next day hunting or left in the waterfowling boat. But we do have a lot of goose decoys including several dozen Avery full bodied decoys. We use a portion of our barn for storage, hanging decoy bags of smaller decoys on the wall, and placing the full bodied and larger bags of field decoys on racks. Since our barn has a gravel floor, old wood skids are used to keep the decoys and bags up off the ground.

One thing you simply can't get enough of is decoy bags. Buy the best you can afford. Not only are they easier to use, but store better and last longer. We've used Avery and Greenhead Gear bags almost exclusively since they were introduced, and the new individual "pocket" bags are fantastic. They not only allow easier setting, retrieving and storage, but these bags also protect the paint and decoys better.

You'll also need a means of storing and transporting other gear including calls, a thermos, lunch and waterproof decoy-retrieving gloves. The Avery Blind bags are unbeatable for this.

Decoys should be stored in a dry, safe place. If you're serious about waterfowling, it takes a lot of decoys and a lot of storage space.

Rigging Box

A simple rigging box such as the one shown can be used to hold weights, crimps and other materials and tools. The dowel on top holds a spool of decoy line and allows you to easily pull off the amount of line needed to quickly and easily rig your decoys. The dowel is glued in a hole bored on the top edge of the box.

A rigging box makes it easy to hold weights, clip-ons and decoy cord for rigging.

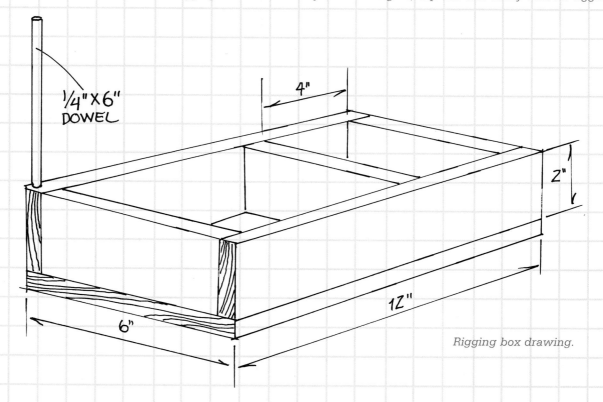

¼" X 6" DOWEL

4"

2"

12"

6"

Rigging box drawing.

Materials

Qty.	Part	Dimensions
2	Sides	³/₄ x 1¹/₄ x 12"
2	Ends	³/₄ x 1¹/₄ x 4¹/₂"
1	Inside divider	³/₄ x 1¹/₄ x 4¹/₂"
1	Bottom	³/₄ x 6 x 12"
1	Dowel	¹/₄ x 6"

Blind Storage

Waterfowl blinds can be permanent or portable. We've gone to portable, packable blinds for the majority of our hunting, and use the Avery blinds. They are quick and easy to set up and you can move almost instantly if you need to. They do require a bit of storage space, and since they're often used in wet, muddy conditions, they should be stored so they can dry out between trips. Standing inside a garage or shed and against a wall is the easiest method, but, if like us you have several, they do take up space, especially during off-season storage. One tactic is to create an overhead cradle of 2 x 4s in a garage or shed and slide the blinds into it for off-season storage. Just make sure the blind is dry before folding up for storage.

Fold-up waterfowl blinds must be allowed to dry before folding up for off-season storage.

DOG GEAR STORAGE

If your hunting dog's food is stored on the back porch, in your garage or other inconvenient location, and the leash, extra collars, dummies, medicine and other gear is stored in another location, you may be interested in this hunting dog storage shed. Located conveniently near my dog pens, this shed holds everything needed in one close-at-hand, tidy spot. The shed is designed to be fastened to the garage wall, next to my dog pens which are also fastened to the rear of the garage wall which also protects them from the north wind. The shed shown doesn't have a back, but a back could be installed to make the shed free-standing. The shed should also have a back if it can't be attached to a flat surface to keep out mice and other pests. The shed shown would be susceptible to toppling over very easily, so should be "staked" or fastened in place in some manner. You will also need something solid to sit the shed on. Concrete blocks, gravel or even a small concrete pad poured of Sakrete would work.

Dog Gear Shed

The siding of the shed shown is hardboard (barn siding) and requires two 4 x 8' sheets. First crosscut 24" off the end of one 4 x 8' sheet. This creates the top. Rip the 6' piece to the correct width for the sides, and then cut their angled ends. Some of the framing is constructed of 2 x 2 ($1\frac{1}{2}$ x $1\frac{1}{2}$") material. The first step is to rip the 2 x 2s from 2 x 4s. Cut the front and back support 2 x 2s to length. Fasten a side down over these framing members. Then measure and cut the bottom and top side pieces to length, making sure the angles are correct on the top pieces. Note the bottom pieces are 2 x 4s. Fasten these between the upright members. All siding should be fastened in place with non-corrosive fasteners. An air brad nailer works great for this step. Repeat for the opposite side.

Stand the sides upright and cut the upper and lower back 2 x 4 cross members to the correct length.

Position the cross pieces between the sides and fasten the sides to them with non-corrosive "decking" screws. Cut and fasten the front 2 x 4 cross members in place in the same manner. Stand the unit upright. Cut and install the floor joists between the front and back lower cross members and then cut and install a $\frac{3}{4}$" floor over the floor joists, notching to fit around the 2 x 2 uprights.

Cut the 2 x 2 door frame members and fit them in place between the front cross pieces. The tops are held in place with a block over the back of the top cross piece and door upright. The bottoms are anchored to a spacer block positioned between it and the side upright.

Use a carpenter's square to make sure the assembly is square. Then rip the front siding pieces and install them in place. Rip the upper and lower siding cross pieces and install them in place.

Materials

Qty.	Part	Dimensions
2	Sides, $\frac{3}{8}$" siding	22 x 72"
2	Side front uprights	2 x 2 x 66"
2	Side rear uprights	2 x 2 x 72"
2	Side bottom cross members	2 x 4 x 19"
2	Side top cross members	2 x 2 x 19"
2	Rear and front bottom cross members	2 x 4 x 42"
2	Front top and rear cross members	2 x 4 x 42"
2	Floor joists	2 x 4 x 19"
2	Rafters	2 x 4 x 19"
1	Floor, $\frac{3}{4}$" plywood	22 x 45"
2	Door frame uprights	2 x 2 x 59"
4	Door frame blocking	2 x 2 x 8"
2	Front siding pieces, $\frac{3}{8}$" hardboard	16 x 66"
1	Upper front siding piece, $\frac{3}{8}$" hardboard	$3\frac{1}{4}$ x 29"
1	Lower front siding piece, $\frac{3}{8}$" hardboard	$3\frac{1}{4}$ x 29"
2	Front upright trim	$\frac{3}{4}$ x $1\frac{1}{2}$ x 59"
2	Side upright trim	$\frac{3}{4}$ x $1\frac{1}{2}$ x 66"
1	Bottom front trim	$\frac{3}{4}$ x $3\frac{1}{2}$ x 42"
1	Top front trim	$\frac{3}{4}$ x $3\frac{1}{4}$ x 42"
2	Door uprights	2 x 2 x $58\frac{1}{2}$"
2	Door inside cross members	2 x 2 x $28\frac{1}{2}$"
2	Door inside upright members	2 x 2 x $58\frac{1}{2}$"
1	Door siding, $\frac{3}{8}$" hardboard	$28\frac{1}{2}$ x $58\frac{1}{2}$"
2	Door upright trim	$\frac{3}{4}$ x $1\frac{1}{2}$ x $58\frac{1}{2}$"
2	Door horizontal trim	$\frac{3}{4}$ x $1\frac{1}{2}$ x $28\frac{1}{2}$"
2	Door cross member trim	$\frac{3}{4}$ x $1\frac{1}{2}$ x 62"
2	Top side trim, cut to angle	$\frac{3}{4}$ x $1\frac{1}{2}$ x 22"
2	Bottom side trim	$\frac{3}{4}$ x $1\frac{1}{2}$ x $20\frac{1}{2}$"
2	Back side trim, angle cut to fit	$\frac{3}{4}$ x $1\frac{1}{2}$ x 69"
1	Top, $\frac{3}{8}$" plywood	22 x 45"
	Shingles to fit	
1	Top back trim strip	$\frac{3}{4}$ x $1\frac{1}{2}$ x 45"
1	Screen door hook	

Dog Gear Shed cont'd

Rip the $1\frac{1}{2}$" trim pieces from a treated 1 x 6. Cut the front uprights to length, making sure their tops follow the angle of the sides. Fasten in place with No. 8d non-corrosive nails. An air nailer, such as the Craftsman utility coil nailer, is perfect for this chore. Cut the upper, lower and back side trim boards and install them in place. Then cut the front top and bottom trim pieces and install them as well.

Cut the door siding piece to size. Then cut the inside uprights from 2 x 2s to the correct length and fasten the siding piece down over the uprights. Cut the bottom and top cross 2 x 2 pieces and fasten them in place. The door also has $1\frac{1}{2}$" trim on the outside. Cut the side door trim pieces to the correct length and fasten in place down over the siding with 8d non-corrosive nails. Fasten the upper and lower cross pieces between them. Angled door cross trim pieces add to the décor. Cut these to fit and fasten in place. Then hang the door and install the hook. You may desire to add a latch, or hasp, if you prefer to have a means of locking the shed.

Cut the interior rafters to size, following the angles of the front and back cross members. One method of doing this is to lay a rafter across the top of the cross members and then use a block of wood held against both pieces to mark the angle on the rafters. Install between the cross members. Install the hardboard top piece for the roof down over the rafters. The top can be left as is, but it's best to apply roll roofing or composite shingles to match an existing building. Then paint or stain to match existing building.

Anchor the completed shed to the outside of a building with screws through the top back cross piece into the building. Apply caulking on the back of the roof edge and to the adjoining building. Finally fasten the top back trim strip down over the caulk and to the shed top and the adjoining building.

A storage shed for dog food, medicine, dummies and collars takes the mess out of your back porch and puts everything close to the dog pen.

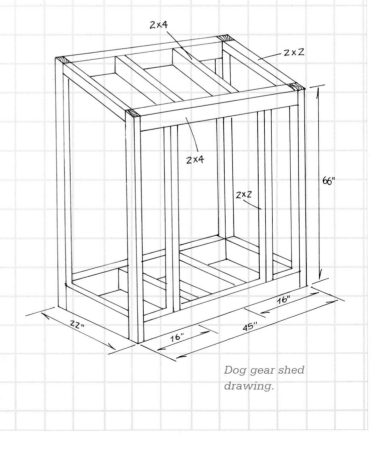

Dog gear shed drawing.

UPLAND AND SMALL GAME GEAR STORAGE

Upland hunters have fewer storage requirements. A place to hang a coat, vest and upland pants, a place for boots and possible storage of ammunition is the basic requirement. The storage cabinet shown is based on a military locker and features a lock so in addition to clothing and gear, you could also store ammunition, or even your favorite upland gun. The locker can be fastened to a wall for further security. In fact, the locker so resembles a military locker, I finished mine in a military gray. The locker should be constructed tightly to prevent wasps and other pests from entering. A vent opening in the door allows clothing stored inside to air out. The vent is covered on the inside with a piece of screenwire. Just don't do as one friend of mine did several years ago and missed a dove in his vest when he hung it up at the end of the season. Two weeks later his wife smelled the remains.

The locker features an inside closet pole and a top shelf. The locker is made mostly of ³/₄" plywood, and you can use economical fir or fancier hardwood plywood such as birch or oak if you prefer a more "finished" look.

A small locking cabinet can be made to hold upland gear, including upland pants and vests, ammunition and other gear.

Upland Cabinet

First step in construction is to rip the sides to the correct width from the plywood, using a table saw or portable circular saw. Then cut the sides to length. Rip the bottom and top pieces to width and cut to length. A $\frac{1}{4}$" rabbet is cut on the inside edges of these pieces to hold a $\frac{1}{4}$" plywood back. Cut this on a table saw, or with a router. An alternative is simply to screw the back to the sides, top and bottom, although the edges of the back will show with that type of construction. (Note: Be sure to allow for this type of back installation when cutting the back and make the back 1" longer and 1" wider.) Fasten the sides to the top and bottom with glue and self-starting wood screws, or if you prefer a more finished look, with finish nails set below the surface and filled with wood putty to match the wood species. Cut the top shelf and install it on 1 x $1\frac{1}{2}$" shelf supports fastened in place with screws into the sides. Make sure the case is square, then cut and add the $\frac{1}{4}$" plywood back, again fastening with glue and screws. Note there is an inside bottom piece as well. This allows setting the door up off the floor. Install this down on the lower bottom piece. If there is a possibility of moisture, you may wish to add small block feet to the bottom. Cut the closet pole to the correct size and install it using closet pole supports. Cut the top and side facers and attach to the front edges of the case with glue and finish nails. Cut the door to fit inside the facers, making sure it is square. Bore the holes for the front vent. Then cover

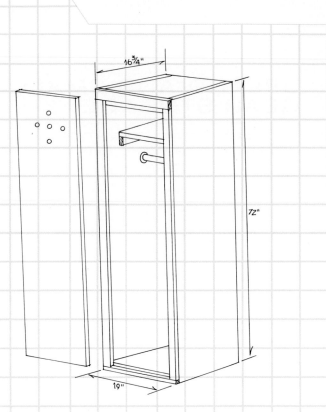

Upland cabinet drawing.

the inside of the vent with a piece of screenwire, held in place with small wooden strips. Then hinge the door in place, mortising the hinges so the door fits tightly, but doesn't bind. Add the padlock and hasp, or you may prefer to use a keyed lock. The latter can be fastened in place by boring a hole in the door and positioning the lock so the back arm swings behind the side facer. Paint or finish to suit.

Materials

Qty.	Part	Dimensions
2	Sides, $\frac{3}{4}$" plywood	16 x 72"
2	Top and bottom, $\frac{3}{4}$" plywood	16 x $17\frac{1}{2}$"
1	Inside bottom, $\frac{3}{4}$" plywood	$15\frac{3}{4}$ x $17\frac{1}{2}$"
1	Back, $\frac{1}{4}$" plywood	18 x 71"
1	Shelf, $\frac{3}{4}$" plywood	12 x $17\frac{1}{4}$"
2	Shelf supports	$\frac{3}{4}$ x $1\frac{1}{2}$ x 12"
1	Closet pole and hanger	17"
2	Side facers	$\frac{3}{4}$ x $1\frac{1}{2}$ x $69\frac{1}{4}$"
1	Top facer	$\frac{3}{4}$ x 2 x 19"
1	Inside top facer	$\frac{3}{4}$ x 2 x $17\frac{1}{2}$"
1	Bottom facer	$\frac{3}{4}$ x $\frac{3}{4}$ x 19"
1	Door, $\frac{3}{4}$" plywood	$15\frac{3}{4}$ x 69"
1 pr.	Hinges	
1	Pull	
1	Lock or hasp	
1	Screenwire	12 x 12"
1	Wire holding strips, cut to fit	$\frac{1}{4}$ x $\frac{1}{4}$ x 48"

Boot Dryer

One essential for upland hunters is a boot dryer. Wet, muddy fields and crossing creeks and ditches can all result in wet boots, and ultimately wet feet. And, the effort needed in all-day walking can also result in sweaty feet and wet boots. Storage space in the bottom of your locker for a boot dryer could be invaluable.

DEER HUNTING GEAR STORAGE

Deer hunters can accumulate a lot of equipment. There's the clothing, including camouflage, raingear and hunter orange. And there are deer scents, deer calls, backpacks and deer stands to store. A locker similar to the upland game locker can be constructed, by simply increasing the size. The locker shown is for our family, which has four hunters. Each hunter has their own locker. The locker is constructed of plywood and features a shelf on top and a closet rod for clothing. A bottom shelf to hold packs with space beneath for boots could also be added, or shelves could be put in the entire cabinet.

Deer Hunter Locker

First step is to rip plywood to create the width needed for the sides, top and outside bottom. Note they are all the same width. Then rip the interior dividers to correct width. Note they are $\frac{1}{4}$" narrower to accommodate the $\frac{1}{4}$" back. Rout or use a table saw to cut the $\frac{1}{4}$" rabbets on the back edges of the top, bottom and sides. Fasten the top, bottom and two sides together on a large, flat, smooth surface such as a garage floor. Use glue and self-starting wood screws. Assemble with the back facing up. Insert the interior dividers in place between the top and bottom pieces and fasten in place with glue and wood screws. Then cut the back from two sheets of $\frac{1}{4}$" plywood. Make sure the assembly is square, using a carpenter's square. Then fasten the back pieces in place with glue and wood screws. Fasten down in the rabbets of the top, bottom and sides and to the interior dividers. Use a string line to mark the locations of the screws from the back into the interior dividers.

Turn the locker over with the front facing up. Cut the shelves and shelf cleats; install the cleats, then the shelves in place. Or you may prefer to utilize adjustable shelving brackets, especially if shelves fill the section. Cut and install the closet rods as desired. Rip and install the top inside facers. Rip the top outside facer and install with No. 6 finish nails. Install the side and other front vertical facers. Set all nails below the wood surface and fill with wood putty.

Cut the doors to the correct size to fit between

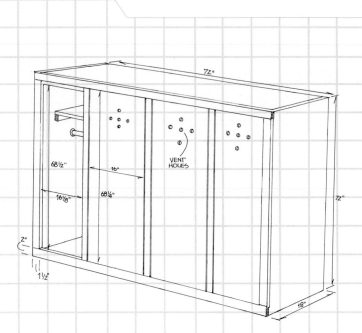

If you have a lot of hunters in the family, especially deer hunters, you may wish to make an enlarged version or military-style "locker."

the facers. Note their tops have holes cut for ventilation. Cut these holes with a forstner bit. Then fasten pieces of screenwire over the vent holes. Install the doors with mortised hinges, cutting the mortises with a handsaw and chisel. You may prefer to install pulls and magnetic catches to hold the door shut, but you may also prefer to install locks. Install locks if you store valuable gear, such as binoculars or ammunition. Or, you may prefer to use simple padlocks and hasp. Finish to suit.

Materials

Qty.	Part	Dimensions
2	Sides, $\frac{3}{4}$" plywood	$17\frac{1}{4}$ x 72"
1	Top, $\frac{3}{4}$" plywood	$17\frac{1}{4}$ x $70\frac{1}{4}$"
1	Bottom, $\frac{3}{4}$" plywood	$17\frac{1}{4}$ x $70\frac{1}{2}$"
1	Back, $\frac{1}{4}$" plywood	71 x 71"
3	Interior dividers, $\frac{3}{4}$" plywood	17 x $69\frac{1}{4}$"
3	Shelves, $\frac{3}{4}$" plywood, cut to fit	12 x $16\frac{1}{2}$"
8	Shelf supports	$\frac{3}{4}$ x $1\frac{1}{2}$ x 12"
4	Top inside facer, cut to fit	$\frac{3}{4}$ x $1\frac{1}{2}$ x $16\frac{3}{4}$"
1	Top outside facer	$\frac{3}{4}$ x $1\frac{1}{2}$ x 72"
1	Bottom outside facer	$\frac{3}{4}$ x 2 x 72"
5	Vertical facers	$\frac{3}{4}$ x $1\frac{1}{2}$ x $68\frac{1}{2}$"
4	Doors, $\frac{3}{4}$" plywood	16 x $68\frac{1}{4}$"
4	Screenwire	12 x 12"
4	Wire holding strips, cut to fit	$\frac{1}{4}$ x $\frac{1}{4}$ x 48"
4 pr.	Hinges	
4	Knobs	
4	Locks or hasps	

Tree Stand Storage

Tree stands should be stored inside during the off season to cut down on rust and corrosion, to protect straps and other fasteners and to prevent theft. Climbing, hang-on and even ladder stands can simply be stood against a garage or shed wall. They're apt to be knocked over, however, and that can be a hassle. Some sort of holder to keep them secured provides a better means of storage. Purchased large garage hanging hooks used for ladders and other gear can be utilized. Handmade, wooden hanging racks, made of 2 x 4s, can also be used to keep the stands secure and safe.

Locking Ammo/Binocular Cabinet

Regardless of whether you are a gun and/or bow hunter, a locking cabinet to hold skinning and hunting knives, binoculars and ammunition can organize items that should be kept locked up. The cabinet shown is made of $3/4$" plywood and has an open shelf below the locking cabinet to hold less valuable gear. Or, you may prefer to make the bottom portion a clothes rack to hold caps and coats. The cabinet shown was to be used in a garage, and the plywood is economical "good one-side" fir plywood. You may prefer to utilize a pine, birch or other more "decorative" plywood if the cabinet is to be installed in a recreation room or trophy room.

First step is to rip the sides, bottom and top pieces to the correct width. Then cut the rabbets in their inside back edges for a $1/4$" plywood back. The shelves are held in place on shelf pins inserted in holes bored in the sides. This allows for a more versatile cabinet in case you desire to add or eliminate shelves, or adjust their heights. Use a combination square to mark a line 2" from each outside edge of the sides. Then mark the shelf pin hole locations. Bore the shelf holes only $3/8$" deep, using a forstner bit in a drill press with the bit set at that depth. Or you can use a stop guide on a bit in a cordless drill, or simply wrap a piece of tape around the drill bit as a "stop-mark." Or you may prefer to use shelf strips with snap-in shelf holders. These are quickly and easily installed. With the sides prepared for shelves, assemble the case on a

A locking ammunition, binocular, hunting knife cabinet can secure these items. The cabinet shown utilizes a simple locking hasp and hidden "Euro"-style hinges.

smooth flat surface. Use glue and self-starting screws, an air nailer or No 6. finish nails. The case should be assembled with the back facing up. Note the bottom ends of the sides extend below the case bottom to

Materials

Qty.	Part	Dimensions
	Sides, $3/4$" plywood	$11^1/2$ x 48"
1	Top, $3/4$" plywood	$11^1/2$ x 33"
1	Bottom shelf, $3/4$" plywood	$11^1/2$ x 33"
1	Case bottom, $3/4$" plywood	$11^1/2$ x 33"
1	Case back, $1/4$" plywood	$33^1/2$ x $33^1/2$"
2	Support cleats	$3/4$ x 2 x 33"
1	Top facer	$3/4$ x $1/2$ x $34^1/2$"
1	Bottom shelf facer	$3/4$ x $1/2$ x 33"
2	Side facers	$3/4$ x $1/2$ x $46^1/2$"
1	Bottom case facer	$3/4$ x $1/2$ x 34"
1	Center divider facer	$3/4$ x $1^1/2$ x 33"
2	Doors, $3/4$" plywood	$16^1/4$ x $33^1/2$"
4	Door edge banding	$1/2$ x $3/4$ x $17^1/4$"
4	Door edge banding	$1/2$ x $3/4$ x $34^1/2$"
3	Shelves, cut to fit	$3/4$ x 10 x $32^1/2$"
12	Shelf pins	
2	Hinges	
1	Lock	
2	Door pulls	

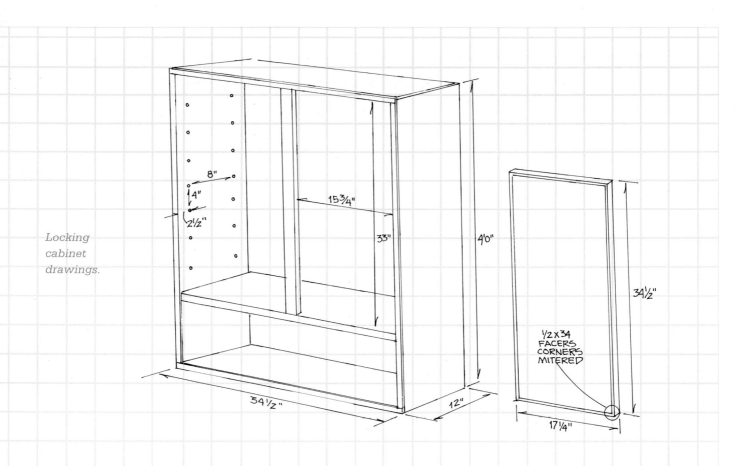

Locking cabinet drawings.

provide for the open shelf or clothes rack. Use a carpenter's square to make sure the case is square. Cut the ¼" back and install it in the squared case using glue and screws into the sides, top and bottom rabbets. Cut the bottom shelf board to width and length and install it between the bottom ends of the sides. Support cleats are used to anchor the cabinet securely to the wall. Cut the support cleats for the inside of the case, one at the top and one at the bottom. Install these between the sides and against the top and bottom boards. Use glue and screws driven from the top and bottom boards into the cleats.

Turn the case over and rip the top facer to width from solid pine 1x material. The facers are ½" thick material to create the Euro-style cabinet. Cut to length and install the top facer piece. Use glue and No. 6 finish nails with the heads set below the wood surface. Fasten the bottom shelf facer board in place in the same manner. Next install the side facers, keeping their outside edges flush with the outside edges of the sides. Then install the bottom case facer between the two side facers, keeping its top edge flush with the bottom top edge. Or you can use edge banding to cover the plywood edges. Install the center di-

vider facer between the top and bottom facers. Use glue and self-starting wood screws driven through the top and bottom facers into the ends of the center divider facer. Fill all nail holes with wood putty and sand the entire case smooth.

Cut the doors to size from ¾" plywood. Note the doors are Euro or full overlay style. The doors also overlay the center divider, providing a means of locking the doors together. The plywood edges are finished off with edge banding, which can be done in one of two ways. You can purchase ready-made edge banding and glue it in place, or you can cut thin wooden strips (½" thick and ¾" wide) and miter their corners, gluing these in place in the same manner as for the cabinet front edges. Sand the door fronts and edge facing smooth.

Apply the finish desired at this time to the case and inside and outside of the doors. Then install the doors using Euro-style hinges. Drill the holes for the locks and install them as well. Add door pulls to the bottom corners. Hang the finished cabinet on the wall in the desired location using self-starting 3" wood screws through the support cleats and into the wall studs.

BOWHUNTING AND ARCHERY EQUIPMENT STORAGE

Bowhunters have many of the same storage requirements as gun deer hunters for stands, optics, packs and other gear. They also require storage for bows, arrows and maintenance tools. A simple bow holder can be made of a piece of $3/4$" stock cut in the shape of a trophy mount board. Insert a $3/4$ x 4" piece of dowel rod at an upward angle. Stain or finish to suit, and then hang the bow over the dowel.

A decorative wall bow and arrow rack can display your favorite bow and arrows and keep them safe and securely stored as well. The rack shown will hold one bow with all accessories intact, including sights, arrow holders, stabilizers and so forth. The rack will also hold a dozen arrows with the broadheads removed. It is made of oak, but could be made of any number of materials. A compartment below the rack features a locking drop-down lid. The compartment provides safe storage for sharp broadheads as well as other archery tackle.

You can make a bow and arrow rack to display your favorite bow and keep it up out of reach. The rack shown is made of red oak.

Bow and Arrow Rack

First step in construction is to enlarge the squared drawing and cut the top back board to shape using a band saw or saber saw. Then enlarge the squared drawing for the sides and cut these to shape as well. Sand all cut surfaces smooth using a drum sander or a dowel with a strip of sandpaper wrapped around it. Cut the top and bottom arrow shelves to length and width. Locate the positions for the arrow holes in the bottom and top arrow shelves. Note they are spaced 2" apart. A router and router table makes the chore easy. Bore these using a forstner bit and drill press or portable electric drill. Then cut the bottom compartment top and bottom pieces to length and width.

Assemble the rack by fastening the top board and bottom top and bottom boards in place between the side pieces. Fasten in place with glue and countersunk wood screws. Then install the compartment top and top and bottom arrow shelves between the sides in the same manner. The bottom arrow shelf sits flush with the back edge of the compartment top board. The top arrow shelf is flush with the back edge of the top back piece. Fasten with glue and wood screws. Cut wood plugs to fill the countersunk screw head holes and glue these in place. Cut the top spacer piece to fit between the sides and glue it in place flush with the outside edge of the top compartment piece. Cut the bottom compartment door to size. Note in the project shown it consists of two pieces for the lock. Or you can use a magnetic catch to hold the door closed, in which case the door can be left as one piece. For the two-piece door, cut to size and rout the outside edge. Then rip $\frac{3}{4}$" off the top edge. Glue this in place to the spacer on top

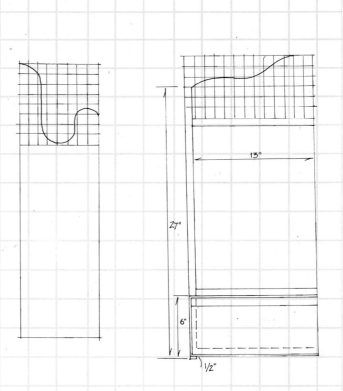

Bow and arrow rack drawings.

of the top compartment piece. Cut mortises in the bottom compartment piece and the door for a set of brass hinges. Sand the case and the door completely. Then finish to suit. The rack shown was made of red oak and finished with three coats of polyurethane varnish, smoothed with steel wool between the coats.

Materials

Qty.	Part	Dimensions
2	Sides	$\frac{3}{4}$ x 8 x 27"
1	Top back	$\frac{3}{4}$ x 6 x 26"
2	Arrow racks	$\frac{3}{4}$ x $2\frac{1}{2}$ x 26"
1	Bottom compartment top	$\frac{3}{4}$ x 8 x 26"
1	Bottom compartment bottom	$\frac{3}{4}$ x 8 x 26"
1	Front shelf spacer	$\frac{3}{4}$ x 1 x 26"
1	Door	$\frac{3}{4}$ x $6\frac{1}{8}$ x $27\frac{1}{2}$"
1 pr.	Hinges	
1	Magnetic catch and door pull or lock	

Arrow Rack

One very simple project to make is an arrow rack for backyard archery practice. The rack is designed to hold a handful of arrows, ready at your side. It consists of a short section of sewer drain pipe with a cap on the bottom, a wooden or metal stake bolted to the pipe and a piece of foam in the bottom of the pipe to protect the arrowhead points. Simply stick the stake in the ground at the chosen distance from the target and place your arrows in it.

An arrow rack for holding arrows during backyard shooting can be made from materials that are easily found.

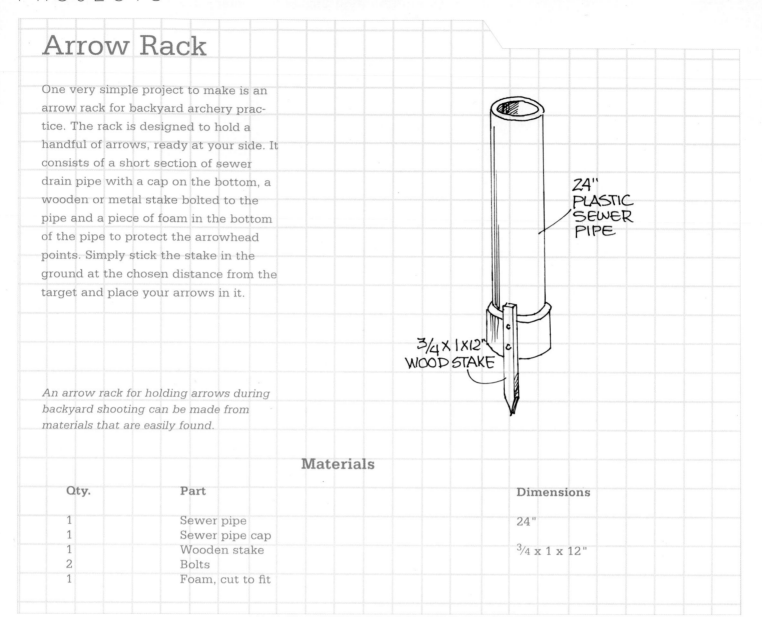

Materials

Qty.	Part	Dimensions
1	Sewer pipe	24"
1	Sewer pipe cap	
1	Wooden stake	¾ x 1 x 12"
2	Bolts	
1	Foam, cut to fit	

Bow and Arrow Making and Maintenance Tools

Constructing your own bow and arrows can be a quite satisfying hobby, but these days, with the popularity of compound bows, bow making is not as common. Assembling your own arrows from shafts, however, is not only a great way of extending the season, but also of creating custom arrows to suit your needs and at a more economical price than purchased arrows. You'll need a fletching cradle, which you can make from wood fairly easily. You may also need a dipping tank if you apply paint to the shafts. The paints used for aluminum shafts is automotive, and a dipping tank can easily be made from a section of water supply line with a cap on it, and a hole in the top to suspend the tank from a nail or hook. You'll also need a fletching jig and feather trimmer if you use real feathers.

Maintenance tools consist of a bow press if you do any repair or adjustments on compound bows. You'll also need a good solid bench to work on.

CHAPTER 4

Stands and Blinds
You Can Build

You can build your own stands and blinds to add to your hunting or just plain wildlife-watching enjoyment. They can also be a lot of fun to build during the off season. I had an old house blind situated on a recycled farm gas tank stand. I called it the Hilton, but my wife Joan said it was more like a cheap highway motel. A couple of years ago our daughter Jodi decided to rebuild the blind. She spent the better part of two Saturdays building her own hunting blind. We then hoisted it in place on the tank stand, bolted it down and the next weekend she shot a dandy buck from her very own house blind.

TURKEY BLINDS

Jodi killed her first tom when she was 10 years old. One of the reasons for her success was a turkey blind. Turkey hunting from a blind offers several advantages. First, it's a great way of concealing an excited youngster. Blinds also offer the chance for

Building your own hunting stands and blinds can be very satisfying. You can build most in a weekend.

more than one person to hunt together and be fairly well concealed. Blinds are great for creating a comfortable hunting spot for younger and older hunters. One old-timer I knew had a thousand acres of hunting property with a dozen blinds located at strategic spots that he had determined over several years of hunting. He knew from experience when and where turkeys would be in specific areas. He simply listened to locate birds, and then went to the blind closest to the gobbling bird. I skeptically sat in one of his blinds one morning until he called in a big tom for me with his well-worn old box call. Another advantage is you can hunt several people in an area without spooking the birds with everyone wandering around hunting. My good friend Ray Eye does this quite successfully with his clients.

The biggest disadvantage to hunting from blinds, as you can guess, is not being where the birds are. If you are sitting in a blind and the birds are in another area, you're in trouble. The answer is a portable blind. We use two types: semi-portable and portable.

Semi-Portable Blind

The semi-portable turkey blind is constructed in much the same manner as a deer hunting shooting house. Constructed of wood, with a camo paint or cloth cover, it has runners on the bottom and can easily be pulled to a location by a four-wheeler or pickup. The blind provides a comfortable, out-of-the-weather place to hunt. The key is placing it in an area turkeys like to use. But, it can also be moved fairly easily.

The blind is constructed of 2 x 4 framing. The floor supports and rafters are left full size; the rest of the framing is ripped into 2 x 2s ($1\frac{1}{2}$ x $1\frac{1}{2}$"). The bottom and top are cut from one piece of exterior or treated $\frac{3}{4}$" plywood. The sides, front and back are cut from $\frac{3}{8}$" treated plywood. The skids are cut from treated 2 x 6s. All pieces are held together with self-starting wood screws. A power drill/driver makes quick, easy work of assembly.

First step is to cut the floor joists to size. Cut the front and rear headers and fasten the floor joists between them. Anchor the bottom to the floor joist

An enclosed semi-portable turkey blind conceals you from sharp-eyed gobblers, and is especially helpful when hunting with youngsters.

Materials

Qty.	Part	Dimensions
2	Front side supports	$1\frac{1}{2}$ x $1\frac{1}{2}$ x $77\frac{1}{2}$"
1	Front top support	2 x 4 x 45"
1	Front bottom support	$1\frac{1}{2}$ x $1\frac{1}{2}$ x 45"
2	Front shelf and window support	$1\frac{1}{2}$ x $1\frac{1}{2}$ x 45"
1	Shelf	$\frac{3}{4}$ x 24 x 48"
1	Front, $\frac{1}{2}$" plywood	48 x $81\frac{1}{4}$"
2	Front window supports	$1\frac{1}{2}$ x $1\frac{1}{2}$ x 12"
2	Front window verticals	$1\frac{1}{2}$ x $1\frac{1}{2}$ x 9"
2	Front window horizontals	$1\frac{1}{2}$ x $1\frac{1}{2}$ x 24"
2	Back side supports	$1\frac{1}{2}$ x $1\frac{1}{2}$ x 72"
2	Back door supports, notched to fit	$1\frac{1}{2}$ x $3\frac{1}{2}$ x 72"
1	Back top support	$1\frac{1}{2}$ x $3\frac{1}{2}$ x 45"
2	Back door verticals	$1\frac{1}{2}$ x $1\frac{1}{2}$ x 68"
2	Back door horizontals	$1\frac{1}{2}$ x $1\frac{1}{2}$ x 33"
4	Bottom floor joists	2 x 4 x 45"
1	Bottom, $\frac{3}{4}$" plywood	47 x 48"
4	Rafters, cut to fit	$1\frac{1}{2}$ x $3\frac{1}{2}$ x 45"
1	Back, $\frac{1}{2}$" plywood	48 x $76\frac{1}{4}$"
1	Top, $\frac{1}{2}$" plywood	48 x 48"
2	Sides, $\frac{1}{2}$" plywood	47 x $81\frac{1}{4}$"
1 pr.	Butt hinges	$1\frac{1}{2}$"
1 pr.	Butt hinges	3"
1 pr.	Screen door hooks	
4	Camo paint colors or camo cloth	

Semi-Portable Blind cont'd

assembly. Rip 2 x 4s for the wall framing. Cut the top slant on the two side walls, and then create the two side walls by fastening the sides in place onto the 2 x 2 framing. Note: Sides are cut to extend down past the bottom to fasten to the outside 2 x 4 floor joist to help anchor the sides. Anchor the side upright. Then anchor the front wall over the front edge of the sides and to the front header between the floor joists. Cut the rear wall to the correct height at the top. Then anchor it to the rear bottom header and to the side walls. Cut the rafters to go between the front and rear wall headers. Anchor them. Then cut the top to fit and anchor. Use a good grade of caulking around the top of the rafters and headers before anchoring the top.

The next step is to cut out the door. Determine the location and use a square and straight edge to mark the door outline. Make sure the bottom edge of the door is at the top of the floor edge. Using a portable circular saw, begin with a pocket cut to cut out the door. You will have to finish the cuts at the corners with a handsaw. Or you can bore starting holes at the corners and use a saber saw to make the cuts. Frame the inside of the door with 2 x 2 stiffeners. Frame the inside of the wall around the door with 2 x 2 stiffeners. Hinge the door and install a screen door hook on both the inside and outside. Place a comfortable chair or stool inside and determine the best shooting height for the windows. Remember, in most instances, you'll be shooting slightly downward or at eye level. Use the same tactic to cut shooting windows in the front and sides. You will also probably wish to cut a small peephole in the back.

The last construction step is to make and fasten the skids. Cut an angle on each end and bore a 1" hole in each end of both skid pieces. Fasten the skids with 3" anchor bolts through the skids into the sides. Bend No. 9 wire into loops of at least two each and thread through the holes. These loops can then be used to pull the blind around with a chain or tow strap.

Paint the entire blind in a midcolor brown then paint a camouflage pattern. The easiest way to provide camouflage is to staple Mossy Oak, a Greenhead Gear camo burlap, over the entire house. Then simply cut shooting slots in the windows. More visibility can be provided through the windows by using Greenhead Gear Die-Cut Nylap.

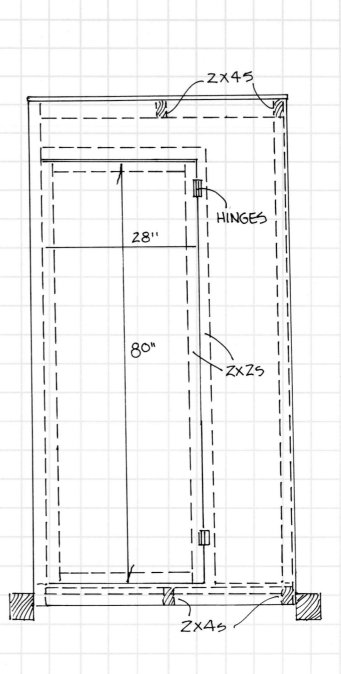

Semi-portable blind drawings.

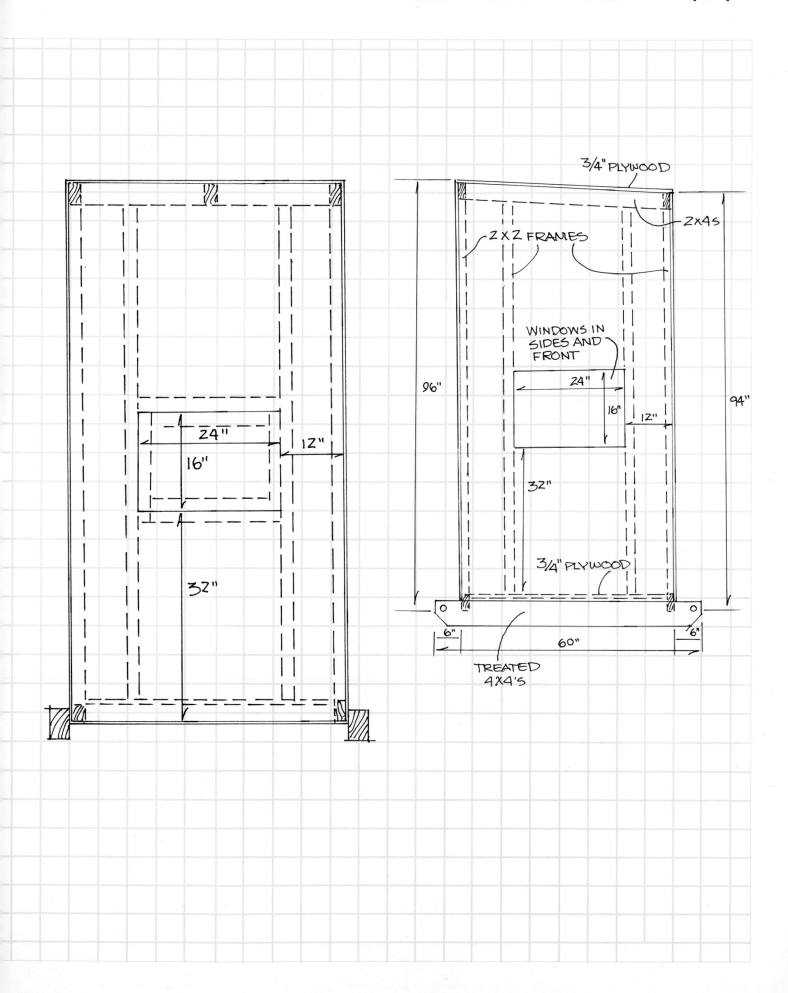

Portable Turkey Blind

A very economical, easy to make and use portable blind utilizes plastic step-in electrical fence posts available at any farm supply house. These are available with notches to hold electric fencing at different heights. They are 48" high and can be cut to suit. Six will make a blind that will easily hide two hunters. The posts come in white or yellow. The first step is to spray paint them a dull brown or green. A lightweight camo cloth such as Mossy Oak Greenhead Gear Die-Cut Nylap or Leafy-Cut Ceretex material 30" high is used as the camo covering. Use 50-pound test fishing line to tie the material to the posts. To use, simply push the posts in place with your foot, creating an arc around the shooting area. The blind can be rolled up and carried wherever you need to hunt. Portable blinds can increase your turkey hunting success. And, it's easy to build your own pull-around, or step-in, carry-style blind.

You can easily build portable, pack-with-you turkey blinds.

Agricultural "step-in" posts are used to hold camouflage netting in place. Spray the posts to camouflage them.

DEER STANDS

"Deer stands sprout like morel mushrooms around here," my wife Joan stated several years ago. And, she was almost right. Each year I add a stand or two to an already fairly large number of existing stands on our property. It seemed with each past deer season I learn new deer use patterns and change some stand locations, but also add more stands simply to be able to hunt prime locations from different wind directions. This really increases the versatility of using prime areas. And, my family grew, along with the list of friends I invited. I had some fairly inexperienced stand hunters along with some hunters with more experience. I needed a safe stand that was fairly economical. As a result, I designed a ladder stand that I could build quickly and easily and for a low cost. It takes only a couple of hours to build a ladder. At the present moment I have a dozen home-built ladder stands scattered around our property. The stands are 12' high, not particularly high for some hunters, but more than enough for others. They're also just about right for the rolling Ozark hills we hunt, but they could be made 14' or even 16' high.

The most important factor is the stands must be made of pressure-treated materials so they won't rot and deteriorate. Also carefully inspect the lumber to make sure there are no weak or splintered spots or knot holes and the boards are full thickness and width. Some more economical treated lumber may be the edge rippings of logs and not be full size.

Over the years I've continued to refine my ladder design. The first stands were assembled using No. 16 galvanized nails which do not rust, so the stands last longer. In the past few years, I've gone to $^3/_8$ x 3" lag screws for fastening the steps in place and $2^1/_2$" brass deck screws for fastening the top seat and braces in place. The two designs include a "fixed seat" and a "hinged seat" design. Note the ladders can be constructed of 2 x 4s or 2 x 6s. The 2 x 6s provide a much stronger stand, especially in the longer lengths, but do weigh quite a bit more.

Deer tree stands are a lot of fun to build, and fairly easy. They must be bolted or screwed together using non-corrosive fasteners and made of sturdy pressure-treated lumber.

Fixed Seat Ladder Stand

Lay the ladder legs out on a smooth, flat surface with the edges up side by side. Locate the positions for the steps and mark these positions on both legs. Use a square to make sure the locations are marked square across the edges of both legs. Cut the steps to the correct length. Position the legs the correct distance for the step lengths. Place the bottom step in position and anchor with one lag screw in each leg. Place the top step in position and anchor it in place with one lag screw in each leg. Use a carpenter's square to make sure the ladder assembly is square, and then install a second lag screw in each step. Locate the position of the remaining steps and anchor them in place.

Cut the seat-board arms to the correct length and angles. Anchor them in place with lag screws through the boards and into the legs. Cut the seat boards to length. Note: A notch is cut in the back to help hold the stand in place against the tree and keep it from sliding sideways. Anchor the seat boards in place with countersunk brass deck screws.

Cut the seat supports and anchor them in place with lag screws into the seat arms and the legs. Add screw bolts for ratchet straps on the insides of the seat arms and on the legs if desired. Paint the stand and apply camouflage patterns if you desire.

I've made a dozen or so of these fairly traditional wooden ladder stands.

Materials

Qty.	Part	Dimensions
2	Ladder uprights	2 x 4" (or 2 x 6") x 12'
2	Seat board arms	2 x 4 x 36"
4	Steps	2 x 4 x 24"
6	Seat boards	2 x 4 x 24"
2	Seat supports	2 x 4 x 30", cut to fit
4	Eye bolts	
2	Ratchet straps	
24	Lag screws	

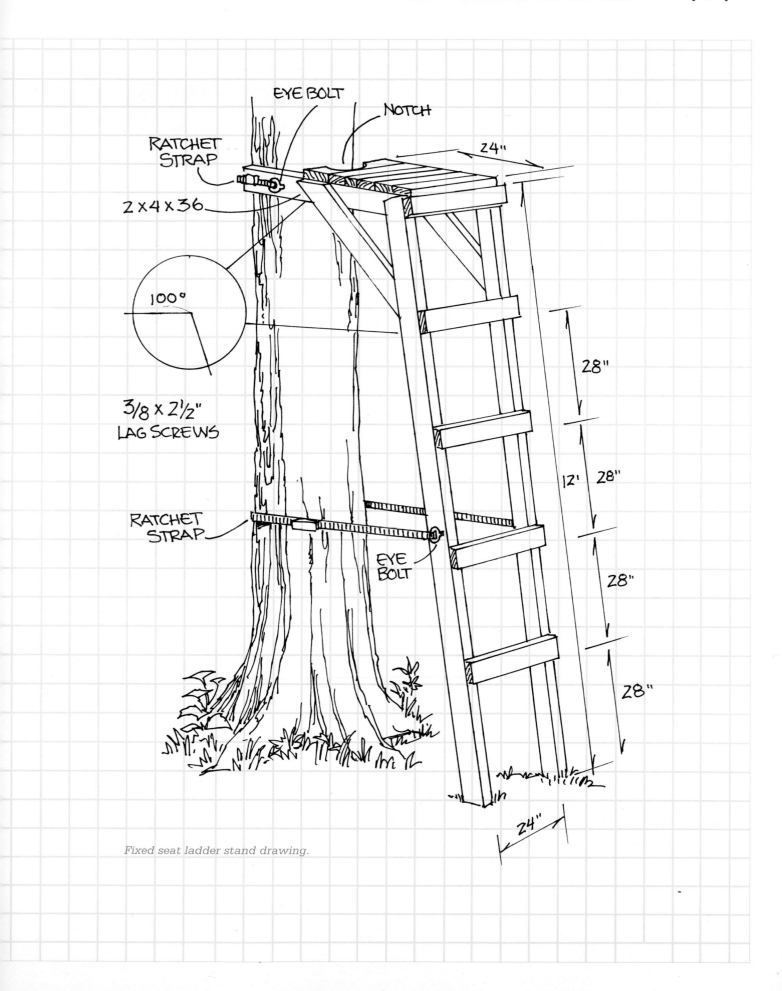

Fixed seat ladder stand drawing.

Hinged Seat Ladder Stand

My nephew Morgan came up with this design, because the angle of the tree and ground doesn't always fit a fixed seat ladder design. The hinged portion allows the ladder to adjust to the angle. The ladder portion is constructed in the same manner as for the fixed seat version and the seat is assembled in the same manner. The seat arms, however, are fastened in place with a ³/₄" threaded rod. It is extremely important with this design that the seat and ladder be positioned properly so it can't "fold" up or down while in place. For added safety, metal braces can be bolted to the seat arms. The opposite ends of the braces are drilled with a series of holes. Bolts are threaded through holes in the legs and through the holes in the arms that best suit the angle. Morgan used his stand last season to collect a good six pointer.

One redesign I've done on some stands is to extend the legs up past the seat arms 2'. A rifle rest bar consists of a 2 x 4 with a bolt through a hole and into one leg. The bar swings down on a bolt on the other leg held in place with a notch cut in the end of the bar.

Although these stands are movable, they require a pickup or trailer to haul around. I like to scout and locate a stand position no later than the weekend before the deer opener and put the stand up at that time. This allows the deer to become used to the stand. This year, however, my daughter Jodi and I put up one stand on a field edge, and then drove past the field and moved an existing stand. When we came back by the new stand, 8 does and a 12-point buck were standing in the field.

You may not need to "sprout" numerous deer stands on your property, but these ladder stands are quick and easy to build and comfortable to hunt from.

My nephew Morgan made a change in his big stand, creating a hinged seat that allows for flexibility in setting up the stand.

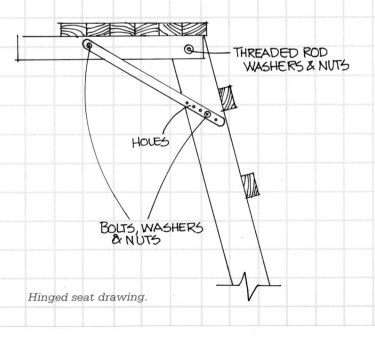

THREADED ROD
WASHERS & NUTS

HOLES

BOLTS, WASHERS
& NUTS

Hinged seat drawing.

Wooden Tree Stand Safety

Wooden stands can be extremely dangerous. Do not use or even test old stands that may have rotted or deteriorated. Even though the wood appears solid, it may be weakened and nails may have rusted. Do not build stands of wood that may rot or deteriorate. Make sure the stand sits on solid ground and does not tip. If necessary, dig down to level one leg. Do not add wood blocks to level the stand. The stand should be at a fairly reasonable angle. It should not be straight up or the feet angled too far out. The first makes for hard and dangerous climbing; the latter may cause the feet to slide outward. Anchor the stand solidly in place. It should be anchored at the seat top using eye bolts and a ratchet strap. These can be purchased in brown or even camouflage colors these days.

Wooden ladder stands can be awkward and hard to put up, especially the higher designs. It's a dangerous chore for one person. Have at least a helper, and two is better to assist in erecting the stand. Lay the stand front down on the ground with the feet in the approximate location. One person should stand on the back side at the feet. One or more people can then lift the seat end, and lifting and reaching to successive steps, "walk" the ladder upright. The person at the rear feet location keeps the feet from sliding as the ladder is tilted upward.

Once the ladder is in place, use a sturdy rope at head height to secure it to the tree. Tie the rope to one leg of the ladder just below a step. Take the rope around the tree and tie it to the opposite leg. You can use a packers knot to pull the rope taunt to hold the ladder top securely against the tree. Or, you can simply use a long ratchet strap to anchor the ladder in place.

One or two persons should continue to steady the stand while another climbs and anchors the top in place. The top should also be secured with a ratchet strap fastened to two screw eyes in the top seat arms.

The number one safety rule, even in a comfortable ladder stand—always use a safety belt.

ARCHERY PRACTICE STAND

Most conscientious bowhunters practice, practice and practice in their backyard, or at a club, flinging arrows at targets every chance they get in the evenings and on weekends before and after the bowhunting seasons. The problem—most everyone practices from the ground, yet hunts from a tree stand that is 12' or higher. The angle of the shot is different, as are the shooting positions. Some bowhunters use their tree stand in the backyard for "real" practice. I've used a ladder stand for that purpose for years. The only problem with tree stands is the time it takes to climb up in them, get your safety belt rigged (you're just as apt, if not more so, to fall in your backyard as in the woods), make a few shots, then climb back down to retrieve the arrows.

The permanent archery stand shown, however, makes elevated practice easy. Simply walk up the steps, make the shots, walk back down to retrieve your arrows.

An archery practice stand at a hunting resort gave me the idea to design this project. It's great for backyard archery practice at an elevated angle simulating shooting out of a tree stand.

Archery Practice Stand

The stand is constructed of pressure-treated materials, including 18' 4 x 4 poles set 3' in the ground. Concrete is poured around the poles to secure them in place. Since it's not always possible to get all holes exactly the same depth, the best tactic for assuring a square, plumb and level assembly is to dig the holes, temporarily set the poles in place and brace them upright. Use temporary cross braces at top and bottom to position the poles at the correct distance and assure they are square with each other. Use a tape measure diagonally from inside to inside of the posts and shift until the measurements are the same to assure a square assembly. Once you have the poles in place and properly braced, mix and pour the concrete around them. Allow the concrete to set.

Self-starting deck screws $2^3/4$" long and a power screwdriver such as the DeWalt 24-volt model make quick and easy work of assembling the tower and provide a long lasting project.

Measure to locate the shortest pole height. Using a straight edge and level, mark that height on the other four posts. Cut off the post tops at that mark. Measure down 3' from the top of the post height. Cut the 2 x 6 side support pieces and fasten in place level

at the 3' mark. Cut the front 2 x 6 support piece and fasten it in place. Cut the two 2 x 6 rear stair support pieces and fasten them in place one on top of the other. Cut a second 2 x 6 "joist" and fasten in position on the inside of the side posts and flush with the top edges of the front and back. Fasten their ends to the front and back. Cut a third center joist and position it in the center and fasten to the front and back support boards.

Cut the cross-braces for all four sides and anchor them in place diagonally, one inside and one outside the support posts. With all joists and cross-braces anchored in place, the next step is to lay the floor. Cut the floor boards to length and position them down on the joists and anchor in place. Note you will have to notch around the corner posts.

With a helper, stand one of the stair stringers in place against the back side. Mark the angle at top and bottom. Or, you can stand the stringer up and temporarily fasten it in place with a screw or nail. Cut the top and bottom ends of the stringers. Cut the stair-step support cleats and fasten in place at the same angle as the top and bottom cuts on the stringers. Then cut all the stair steps. Anchor them in place

Materials

	Qty.	Part	Dimensions
A	4	Support posts	4 x 4" x 18'
B	2	Top side supports	2 x 4 x 48"
C	2	Lower side supports	2 x 6 x 51"
D	1	Top front support	2 x 4 x 51"
E	1	Lower front support	2 x 6 x 48"
F	2	Side top rails	2 x 4 x 49½"
G	1	Front top rail	2 x 4 x 41"
H	8	Side, front and back braces	2 x 4 x 12'
I	2	Stair stringers, cut to fit	2 x 10 x 16'
J	24	Stair support cleats	2 x 2 x 9"
K	12	Stair steps	2 x 10 x 45"
L	1	Top stair stringer support board	2 x 6 x 45"
M	2	Bottom stair support posts	4 x 4 x 8"
N	2	Stair rails	2 x 4 x 16'
O	2	Center stair supports, cut to fit	2 x 4 x 3'
P	9	Flooring	2 x 6 x 51"
Q	3	Floor joists	2 x 6 x 48"
R	2	Rear stair supports	2 x 6 x 48"

Archery Practice Stand cont'd

with screws down into the supports and from the sides of the stringers into the step ends. Cut a 2 x 6 to fit between the stringers and fasten to the upper end, inside the stair stringers, as an anchor into the platform. Stand the assembly up and temporarily fasten in place at the upper end to the tower. Move the bottom end of the stair assembly around until it is square with the rest of the tower. Mark locations of the bottom posts. Then swing the platform off to one side and dig the bottom rail support post for that side. Move the bottom to the opposite side and dig that hole. Then reposition the stair assembly square with the platform and position the posts in place. Fasten the bottom of the stair assembly to the posts, making sure the posts are plumb. Pour concrete around the posts and allow to cure.

Once the posts have set, fasten down the floor boards. Note they must be cut to fit around the posts. Anchor the top of the stair stringer system in place to the back of the platform. Then cut the top rails and anchor them in place. Hold a 2 x 4 stair rail in place and mark the angles on both ends, then cut. Anchor to the top of the platform rail and to the lower post. Then install the single rail supports on each side.

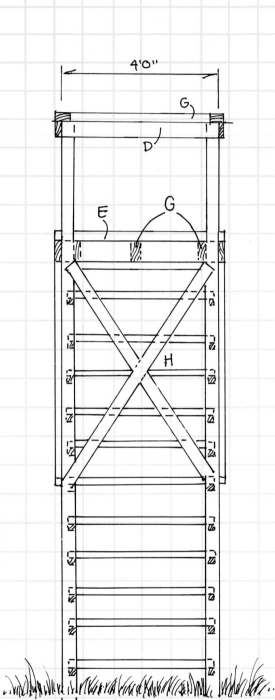

Archery practice stand drawings.

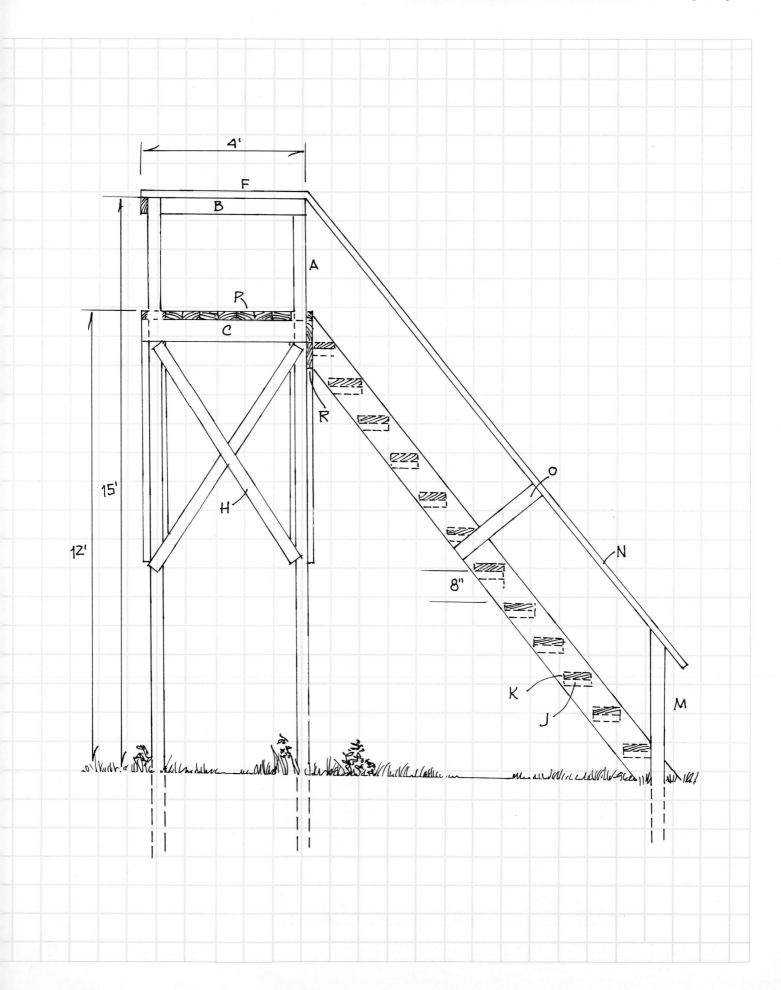

HOME-GROWN CLAY SHOOTING

It's been a tradition in our family for years. After a morning of scouting for birds, Saturday afternoon of the weekend before dove season is spent busting clay pigeons. We began many years ago with a simple hand-trap, and that is still the most economical. We then graduated to a Trius foot trap, and we still use it for portable and informal shooting. In those days we usually threw targets in the same manner as trap. Then came sporting clays and things became quite different.

Adding shotgun shooting games to your off season can add to the fun. Not only are these games a great way to sharpen your eye for hunting, they can provide friendly competition and a great way to while away time when you're not hunting. Shotgun games are great fun for the entire family and a way of getting the families involved in hunting. These games are also a great way of teaching youngsters shotgunning skills.

Shotgun games can be as structured as trap, skeet or sporting clays, or five stand using multiple traps. Or they can be informal with the simplest of traps. A lot depends on the amount of time, money and property you wish to invest.

Sporting clays is an extremely popular shooting sport. You can make up your own portable sporting clays shooting station and move it as needed to set up your own course.

The most popular game these days is sporting clays, a challenging clay target game designed to simulate field shooting. On a sporting clays course shooters are presented with a wide variety of targets simulating the flight paths of game birds, such as flushing, crossing, incoming and other angling shots. The courses are laid out in natural surroundings typically with five to ten shooting stations. The shooters move from one station to the next to complete the course. Each station presents the shooters with a different type of shot.

Unlike trap and skeet, where a mounted gun is permitted, sporting clays courses require the shooter start out with a "low gun" (butt of gun below the shoulder) until the target comes into full view. A full round of sporting clays usually consists of 50 to 100 targets (it depends on the number of stations, sometimes a tournament may require up to 13 to 15 stations) with 10 targets normally thrown at each station. (Some tournaments may lessen the number of birds pulled if there are more stations but the targets always add up to 100.) When shooting in squads, shooters typically rotate turns from station to station. At most stations shooters call for each target or targets, which may be released with up to a three-second delay.

For more information on rules and regulations and setting up a clays course, contact: National Sporting Clays Association, 5931 Roft Road, San Antonio, TX 78253, 800-877-5338, 210-688-3371, www.nssa-nsca.com.

Setting up a permanent, home-grown clays course for your friends and family doesn't have to be as regulated as for public courses, unless you desire to hold National Sporting Clays Association tournaments. The number of stations and the types of "birds" thrown depends on your property—the amount of property available as well as the terrain and cover. The idea is to simulate different field hunting situations. The first consideration is safety. The course should be set aside in an area away from other activities and with plenty of room around the exterior to avoid falling shot. The entire course, as well as the perimeter, should be well marked with warning signs to prevent someone from straying into the shooting zones.

Try to provide a variety of hunting situations. For instance, a grouse station would have the shooters facing birds flushing in and out of trees. At a decoying duck station, targets are thrown to provide incoming shots floating over a pond. One club I hunted even had you sit in a boat permanently stationed on the bank of the pond. Rabbit stations are extremely popular. Special targets are thrown on end and they skitter and bounce across the ground. To make this even more challenging, space hay bales in front of the target's course so shooters have to shoot as the target bounces between the bales. Wooden cages are positioned at each station to "guide" the shooter toward the target zone, protect the thrower and prevent the shooter from shooting out of a safe zone.

To further add challenge, target size may vary from the standard trap/skeet clay bird to smaller "midi" and "mini" targets, rabbit or a flat disc shaped "battue" target.

You don't even need to have a permanent setup for informal shooting fun. Almost any area can be made into a "hunter's" clays area. Again, make sure of the backstop or background for safety. Several years ago I came up with a portable style of "home-grown clays," utilizing only one or two portable traps and a portable shooting cage to direct shots and protect the trap thrower. The cage is constructed in much the same manner as for permanent clay course cages, except it's made to be dismantled and transported in the back of a pickup or SUV. This, as well as the trap thrower, can be moved to different locations quite easily to create a variety of shooting situations.

The station consists of two panels covered with lattice and a solid back panel held together with bolts and wing-nuts.

The entire station is easily moved around.

Clay Shooting Station

The cage consists of three pieces—a solid back piece and two open side pieces. The back is solid so the clays thrower can throw from behind to either side or even overhead to create going away shots without endangering the shooter with the targets. The open grill sides keep the shooter pointed in a safe zone in relation to the thrower, limit the angle of side shots, but allows for side vision of the targets thrown. The three pieces are held together with interior door hinges with removable pins. This allows you to swing the sides in or out to stabilize or make different shooting zones. To dismantle, simply pull the pins on the hinges.

One of these cages and a decent trap can be used to create a variety of shooting situations very economically. For even more variety and protection for the thrower, make a two-piece folding trap house. The hinged pieces are set with one side to the shooter and one to the back with the front open. This also helps conceal the action of the thrower from the shooter.

The most common method is to have the thrower on either side of the shooter, throwing out front or to either side. The next option is to have the thrower situated to either side throwing crossing shots. Then you can move the thrower to the back of the shooter. Add in terrain, trees, brush and other obstacles to create more challenge and fun. Be inventive. Years ago when my grandad still had his old hay-loft barn, we threw targets out the loft door for high overhead shots. And, we threw targets from one side of the barn over to the shooter on the opposite side.

Regardless of how you set up a portable or informal shotgun shooting game, make sure you follow all safety rules. Position the thrower and shooter where there is no danger to the thrower, shooter or other persons, farm animals, buildings or other objects. Of course, you'll need traps for throwing targets. Although commercial electric traps can run into thousands of dollars, a number of economical traps can be used for permanent ranges. Many of these are also very portable, and can be used to create "instant" clays or "hunter's clays" courses. Trius Products has a line of very economical traps for those wishing to create portable courses. For over 45 years the Trius Original Foot Trap has been a best seller. Designed to be held in place with a foot or mounted to a tire, the trap can be adjusted to throw a variety of angles, doubles and even piggy-back doubles. Their 1-Step Trap is even easier.

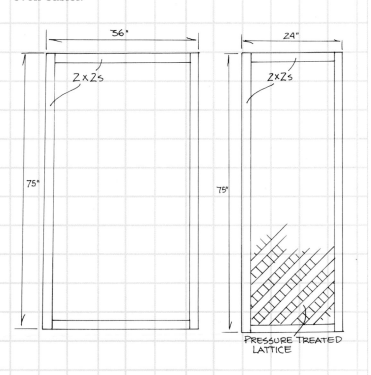

Portable clay shooting station drawing.

Materials

Qty.	Part	Dimensions
2	Back uprights	2 x 2 x 75"
2	Back top and bottom	2 x 2 x 33"
1	Back center piece, ¼" plywood	36 x 75"
4	Side uprights	2 x 2 x 75"
4	Side top and bottom	2 x 2 x 21"
2	Side center lathes	24 x 75"

SHOOTING HOUSE

Shooting houses provide the ultimate in deer hunting comfort. Not only do they shelter you from the weather, they can also provide a shooting rest for more accurate shots. Properly constructed and used, shooting houses can also help contain human scent. Houses are usually placed permanently on the edges of green fields, food plots, overlooking power lines or other clearings. Many such houses have been in the same location for years, with numerous successful hunts the result. Permanent houses, however, can be a problem if not located properly. More than one landowner hunter, myself included, has wished their shooting house was in a different spot. The answer—a portable house on skids. When my wife took up deer hunting after our youngest flew the coop, she and I hunted out of one of my old houses, and she took her first deer, a big fat doe. We soon discovered the houses were just too small for two people, and all were permanent. So we built "The Hilton" as she dubbed it, a pull-around house, and placed it on the edge of a clover/alfalfa food plot. She took an antlerless deer the first morning of the season and a 10-point buck, her first buck, the

A shooting house can not only provide comfort for day-long hunting, but keep game from seeing and smelling you. The house shown is elevated, but can be pulled around with a tractor or truck.

second morning. Believe me, "grandma" is getting into this deer hunting.

The pull-around house is positioned on skids, but sits high enough to provide a good view. I pulled the house in place with my tractor, but a pickup or even a heavy-duty ATV could be used. The house is also designed to slide into a 6' wide utility trailer for transporting. With today's powerful battery-powered electric tools, however, you could build the house at camp, or near the hunting site.

I didn't get the house built and moved into place until the weekend before the deer opener. Deer had been using the field extensively and they never stopped.

Shooting House

The house takes a little time to build. You should plan on two weekends by the time the house is painted, camouflaged, in place and ready to hunt. A friend can be a great help in lifting and holding boards and sheets of siding. It is extremely important that the house be constructed on a flat and level site.

A hammer, handsaw, level, tape measure and carpenter's square, ratchet or open-end wrench are essential. I used a Craftsman 18-volt cordless electric drill, a DeWalt 24-volt cordless portable circular saw and a Makita cordless saber saw. I also used a new tool, the Craftsman Accu Rip, to rip and trim the siding panels as well as a Craftsman Speed Lok set,

which combines a drill bit and driver set in one unit for instant changing of bits.

All exposed wood is pressure treated for long life, and brass or galvanized exterior self-starting wood screws were used for the majority of the fastening. Total cost of the house shown is approximately $400, using new materials throughout.

First step in construction is to cut the skids to length, then round the ends. The ends are rounded using a saber saw or by making successive angled cuts with a portable circular saw. Fasten two upright posts to the inside of one with lag screws, placing the posts up 2" from the bottom edge of the skid. Use a

Materials

Qty.	Part	Dimensions
2	Skids	2 x 8" x 8'
4	Inside skid support blocks, cut to fit	$1\frac{1}{2}$ x $7\frac{1}{2}$ x $7\frac{1}{2}$"
2	Front posts	4 x 4" x 10'
2	Rear posts	4 x 4" x $9\frac{1}{2}$'
2	Side joists	2 x 6 x 45"
2	Front and rear joists	2 x 6 x 72"
2	Center joists	2 x 6 x 45"
1	Floor	$\frac{3}{4}$ x 48 x 72"
2	Outside rafters	2 x 4 x 48"
2	Rafter hangers	2 x 4 x 72"
4	Front and rear bottom braces, cut to fit	2 x 4 x 72"
4	Side bottom braces, cut to fit	2 x 4 x 48"
2	Skid braces	2 x 6 x 72"
2	Step stringers, cut to fit	2 x 8 x 36"
2	Steps	2 x 6 x 30"
2	Inside rafters, cut to fit	2 x 4 x 48"
2	Studs, front	2 x 4 x 84"
3	Studs, rear	2 x 4 x 78"
2	Studs, sides, cut to fit	2 x 4 x 84"
1	Cripple stud, upper	2 x 4 x $30\frac{1}{2}$
1	Cripple stud, lower	2 x 4 x $34\frac{1}{2}$"
2	Window frames, front	2 x 4 x 32"
4	Window frames, side	2 x 4 x 18"
2	Window frames, rear	2 x 4 x 10"
4	Corner blocking, cut to fit	2 x 4 x 84"
4	Corner blocking, cut to fit	2 x 2 x 84"
5	Siding, $\frac{1}{2}$" plywood	4 x 8' x $\frac{1}{2}$"
1	Top, $\frac{1}{2}$" plywood	4 x 6'
1	Door, cut to fit	6'2" x 30"
	Hinges and knob or latches to suit	
	Plexiglas windows: front, rear and sides, cut to fit	
8	Butt hinges	1"
16	Lag bolts $\frac{1}{2}$ x 4"	
12	Exterior self-starting wood screws	No. 10 x $2\frac{1}{2}$"
	Camo paint and camo cloth	

Shooting House cont'd

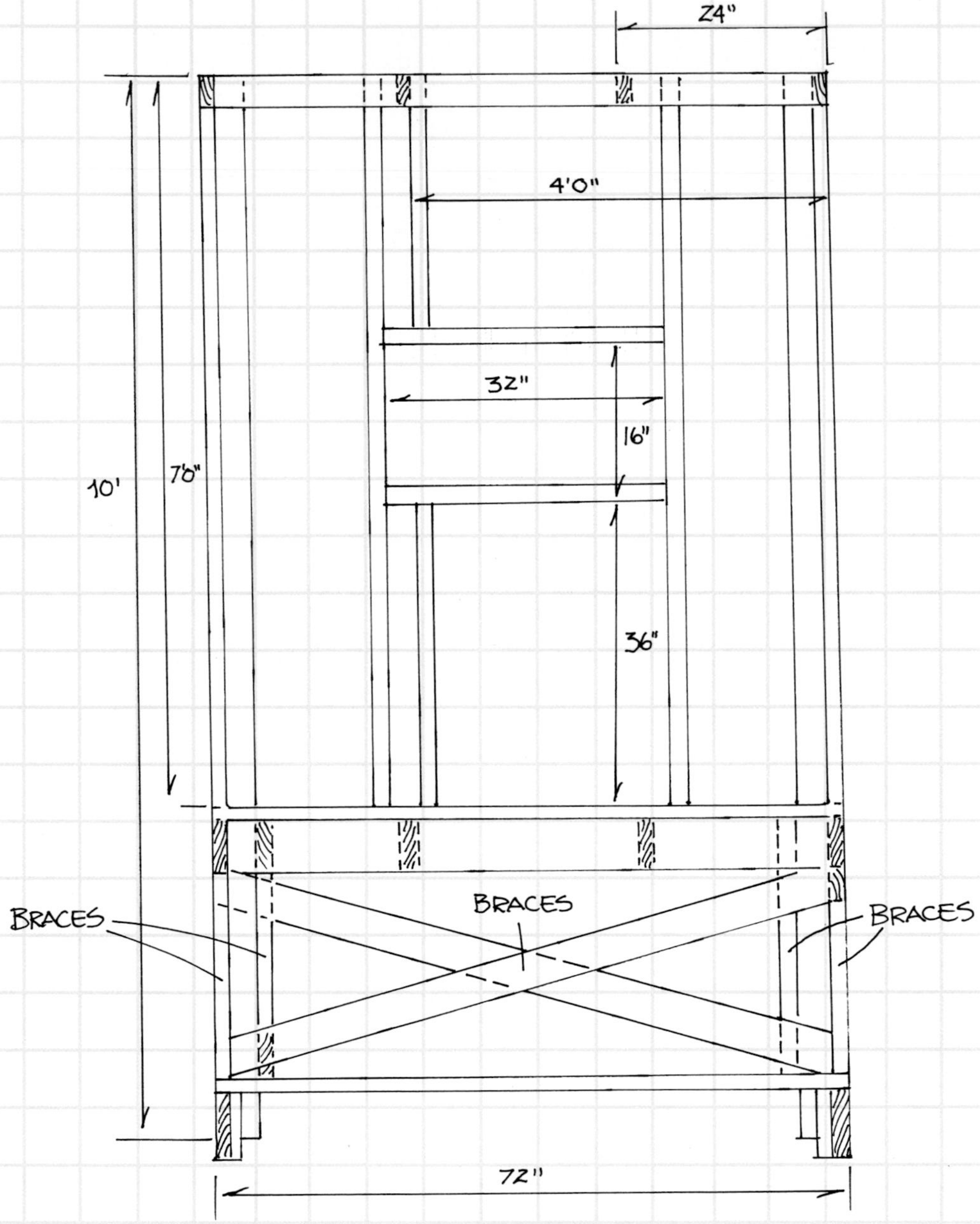

24"

4'0"

32"

16"

10'   7'6"

36"

BRACES

BRACES

BRACES

72"

Shooting house measurements.

Front View

carpenter's square to assure the upright posts are square with the skid. Cut a side joist to length and attach it to the posts, also making sure it is square. Then cut an outside rafter, cutting the ends to the correct angle. Fasten the outside rafter to the posts, positioning it so none of the edges of the posts protrude above the rafter. Repeat these steps for the opposite side assembly.

Now a friend would be greatly appreciated. Fasten one end of the front joist to one side assembly, making sure all is square. Then stand the assembly up along with the opposite side assembly and fasten the front joist to that side as well. Fasten the back joist to both side assemblies. It is extremely important at this step to level and plumb the entire as-

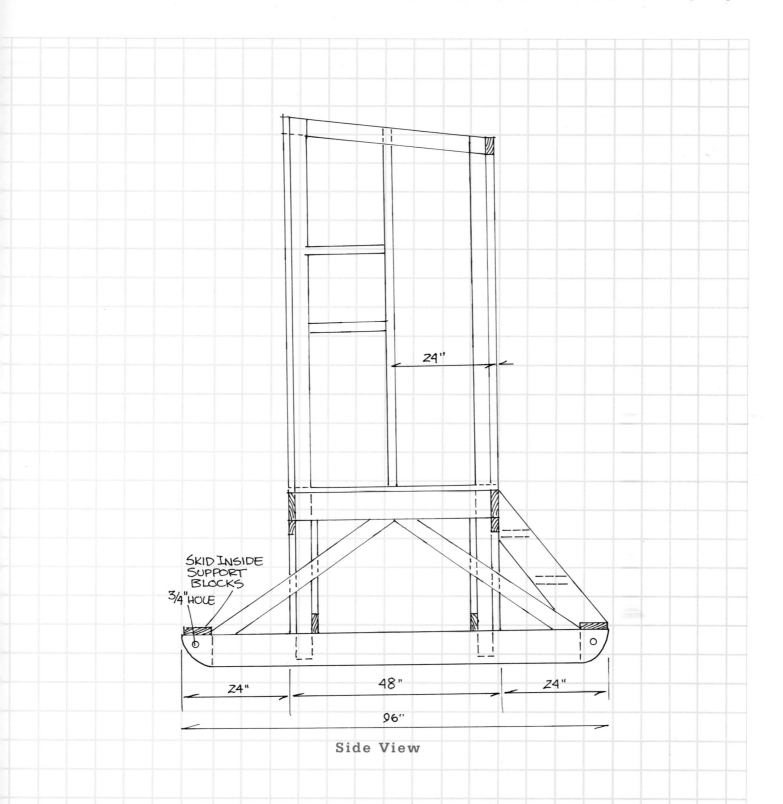

SKID INSIDE
SUPPORT
BLOCKS

3/4" HOLE

24"

24"   48"   24"

96"

Side View

sembly. Use shims or wedges under the corners of the skids if necessary to make sure they are absolutely level.

Cut the two inside floor joists to the correct length and fasten them between the front and rear joists. Cut the floor to the correct size. Note the floor fits to the outside edges of the floor joists. Cut notches in

each corner of the floor to fit around the posts. Position the floor in place and fasten it down.

Cut the front and rear rafter hangers and fasten them to the top edges of the uprights. Then cut the rafters to fit between the rafter hangers.

Cut the front and rear skid braces and fasten them in place. Cut the 2 x 4 side, front and rear bot-

Shooting House cont'd

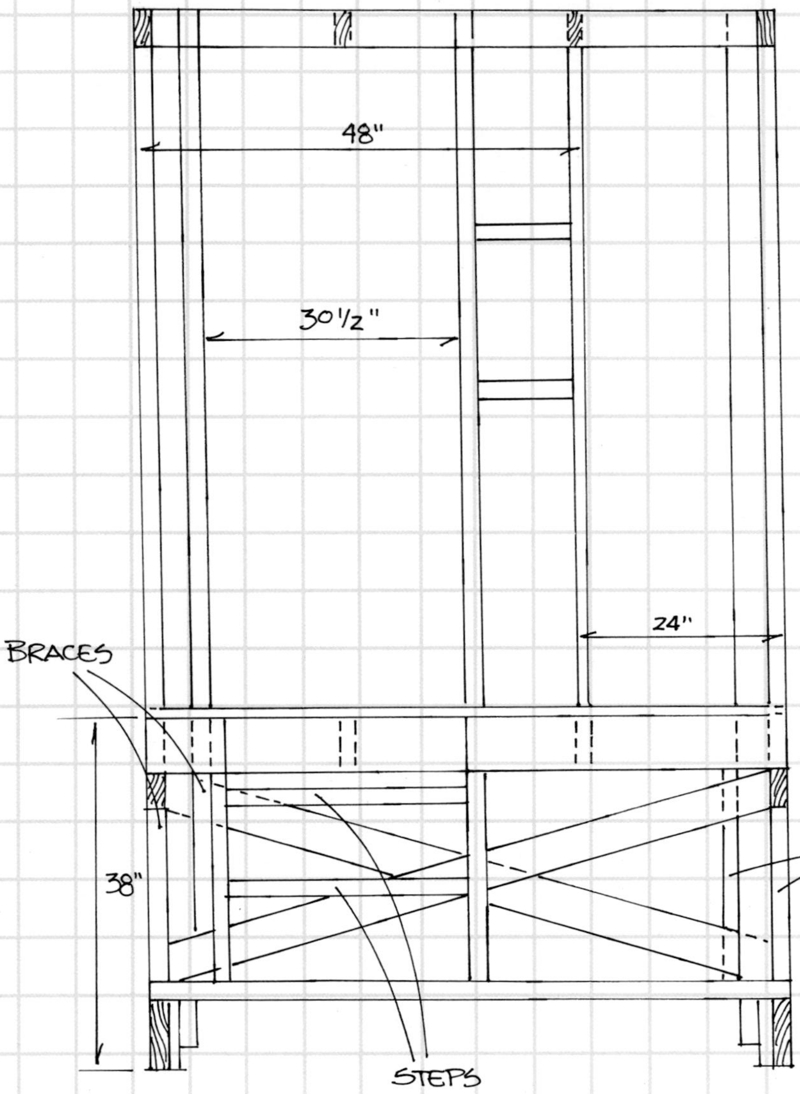

48"

30½"

24"

BRACES

38"

BRACES

STEPS

Rear View

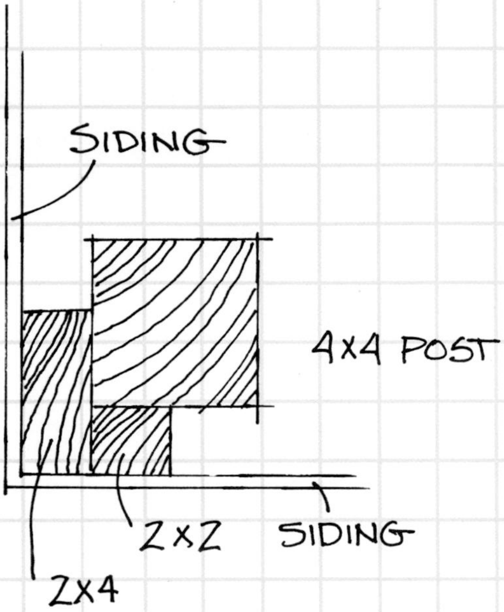

SIDING

4X4 POST

2X2   SIDING

2X4

Above: Making the corner blocking.

Left: Steps installed below the rear doorway.

tom braces and install them in place. Cut the step stringers to the correct length, cut the bottom and top angles and fasten in place. Cut the steps to fit and install them.

Cut the studs and fasten them in place, notching them to fit around the outside rafters and front and rear rafter hangers. Small blocks can be fastened to the floor to help anchor the studs to the floor. Cut and

install the corner blocking, ripping two 2 x 4s to create the four 2 x 2s needed. Then cut the window top and bottom framing and install between the studs. Cut the cripple studs that fit above and below the window frames and install in place.

Cut and install the siding pieces. Mark the locations for the window openings. Using a drill and bit, drill a hole from the inside at each window corner. Use

It will take at least a couple of weekends to build this fairly extensive house. And you'll probably appreciate a friend's help.

a straight edge and pencil to mark between the holes outlining the windows. The simplest way to cut the window openings is to use a saber saw. Insert the saw blade into the drilled holes and cut on the marked lines. You can also use a circular saw to make pocket cuts. Hold back the blade guard on the circular saw with the guard tab. Position the front of the saw shoe on the wood surface and start the saw. Slowly and carefully lower the saw blade into the wood and follow the marked lines for the window opening. Stop the saw at each corner and use a handsaw to complete the cut.

Cut the top piece to the correct size and fasten the top securely in place. The top should be sealed with caulking around all edges. The top can be further waterproofed by coating with an asphalt based roof coating or using pieces of asphalt roll roofing and sealing the edges with tubed asphalt sealant.

I used an old door, cutting it to fit and installing it using butt hinges and an exterior lock. You can also use the piece of siding cut for the opening and strengthen the edges with 2 x 2s to create a door, or purchase a new or used door.

Cut the inside skid support blocks and fasten in place with screws. Note, the grain on these blocks must be opposite the grain on the skids. Then bore holes through the skids and support blocks. I used a piece of aircraft cable and cable clamps to create a tow for the house.

The entire house should be given a coat of dull flat paint to match the base surrounding colors. Brown for deciduous woods, green for pine. Then comes the fun of camouflaging. Light tan, brown, black and green flat exterior spray paints are used to provide the camouflage pattern. One method is to spray a pattern of tan in blobs and streaks. Then hold a piece of plastic leaf or fern against the tan and spray over it with the darker colors.

The windows are covered with mesh camouflage from the inside and shooting slits cut in the mesh. Another method is to place Plexiglas windows on hinges inside. These windows can be dropped down, or hinged to swing up as needed, and in colder climates the covered windows would definitely be a plus.

Tools

It requires carpentry tools to build the stands and blinds. You can build most of them with nothing more than a hammer, screwdriver, tape measurer, square and saw. Cordless portable power tools are the wonder these days, and a wide variety of tools are available that can make building these and many other outdoor project chores easier and much better. This includes: cordless drill/drivers, impact drivers, jig saws, reciprocating saws, portable circular saws and even miter saws. Black & Decker even has a cordless pole tree pruner that can make short work of trimming overhanging branches away from stands and blinds. I've had the opportunity to test most of the new cordless tools as they have come out. What began as small volts is now available in volts up to 36. And, battery power and ease of charging makes these tools day-long wonders. I've used many all day long for framing buildings away from electricity. The Black & Decker Firestorm drill offers 36 volts of power that will handle any drilling and driving chores. The Craftsman impact driver can make short work of any screwdriving operation, and it features a light for easy visibility in dark areas. Bosch offers a full line of excellent cordless tools, including their 18- and 24-volt cordless circular saws. One of the more unusual tools is the Bosch miter saw. It's like having a contractor's miter saw right on the job without the cord. The Milwaukee V28 line of cordless tools is awesome in power using lithium-ion batteries. The two I've tested include their reciprocating saw and cordless circular saw. When you need to make circular cuts, the Makita cordless jig saw is easy and fast. And Black & Decker as well as Paslode both offer cordless air nailers for fast assembly of projects.

You'll need carpenter's tools for building projects such as stands and blinds. A wide range of cordless power tools can make the chore easier, faster and better.

CHAPTER 5

Boating, Camping, and ATV Storage and Equipment

Boats and ATVs are major investments. Storing and maintaining them properly can not only protect your investment, but provide easier, more enjoyable and safer use. Storage can run from outside to inside. Camping equipment can range from backpacking gear with minimal storage and gear to full auto camping for a whole family with lots of sleeping bags, coolers, stoves, food supplies and other gear. When it comes to camping, the more organized you are in storage, the easier it is to go camping. In fact, serious campers keep a gear and supply list next to the storage area, checking off gear and supplies as they are loaded for the campsite.

BOAT STORAGE

Properly storing your boat through the winter season is extremely important in order to maintain your investment. How you do it depends on your geographical location, and how much or whether you use your boat during the winter months. If you live in the hardwater country of the North, you're probably looking at four months or more down time. If you live in the South, or even the lower Midwest, as I do, there's usually open water and some great fishing throughout the winter months. Northern winters can be brutal with deep-freeze temperatures and heavy snow loads. Extra precau-

Properly storing boats, ATVs and camping gear is extremely important for the longevity of your investment. This definitely isn't the way to do it.

tions should be taken to protect your boat, motor and equipment. If possible, store inside, but this is often not feasible. Following is a checklist for proper storage. You might wish to copy it and check off as you do each chore.

1. Remove all electronics and move to a safe, warm, but not hot, and dry storage area. Make sure to remove any liquids, such as fish attractants, unused drinks, etc. Remove the fire extinguisher and all PFDs.

2. You may also wish to remove batteries, if possible, and store them with your other gear. Do not store them on a concrete floor as it will zap the energy. Regardless, make sure they have a full charge before storing. If you can't remove the batteries, disconnect electrical connections.

3. Open all compartments and prop lids to provide ventilation. Place a few moth-balls in open plastic containers to discourage mice, squirrels and other rodents.

4. It's a good idea to remove all tackle and rods as well.

5. If the trolling motor is the plug-in, easy-removal style, unplug and remove it. Or unplug and coat the plug with an anti-corrosion oil or grease.

6. Check the bilge area and drain all water. Leave the drain plug out. Drain and check all livewells and make sure the lines are drained as well.

7. It's a good idea to wash and wax the boat, clean the upholstery and interior. This will help protect the boat and provide a clean, ready-to-go boat in the spring.

8. Check all electrical wiring. Replace any wires or other components that are damaged.

9. You have two choices with fuel tanks. Portable fuel tanks can be removed and stored separately. Regardless of whether portable or inboard, it's a good idea to fill the tank and add a fuel conditioner/stabilizer such as Gold Eagle Sta-Bil concentrated fuel stabilizer. This prevents fuel oxidation, gum and varnish deposits and inhibits corrosion.

10. Coat all engine parts with engine-fogging oil. This helps prevent rust from moisture and acidic combustion in two-cycle engines during extended storage. It's a good idea to run a bit of the treated gasoline through the outboard. Make sure

you follow the fogging oil manufacturer's instructions. The fogging oil should be used while the engine runs for 30 seconds or so as well. You can do these two steps at the ramp before you pull the boat out for the winter. But an outboard flush adaptor hooked to a garden hose and placed over the lower unit can be used. Never run water-cooled outboards without water circulating through them.

11. If your outboard is an older model, you may also wish to completely drain and replace the fluid in the lower unit. Any water in the gearcase can freeze, causing serious and costly damage.

12. Clean the outboard, wax it and apply grease to the fittings.

13. Apply a silicone protectant and lubricant to the entire engine, under the cowl and to protect other metal, rubber and plastic parts from corrosion and rust.

14. Remove the prop and lightly grease the shaft. Inspect for any dents or damage. It's easier to replace a prop now than in the hectic hurry of early-spring fishing.

15. Inspect the wheels and bearings on the trailer. Repack bearings if they are older. A bad seal can allow water to get into the bearings in the winter, rust forms and next spring you'll be sitting alongside the road instead of fishing.

16. Touch up rusted areas on the trailer.

17. Examine the wiring and replace or rewire any loose connections. Could save you a traffic ticket next spring.

18. Lubricate winch and check the strap. Replace if necessary.

19. Check the tires for wear, and if necessary replace them or have them balanced. If possible, jack the boat/trailer up and block it to remove weight from the tires during storage.

20. One of the most important winterizing steps is to cover the boat. If possible, use a boat cover custom fitted to the boat. Even if you do, you may wish to cover that with a tarp as well to protect the cover, and add more weather protection. One of the problems is heavy snow or rainwater collecting on a sagging boat cover. It then pools, is hard to remove and may eventually work under the cover into the boat. Make sure the cover is taut, and provide additional support in

areas where it may sag. One new winterizing option these days is do-it-yourself shrinkwrapping, such as that from Dr. Shrink. It is more cost effective and provides better protection from the harsh winter conditions than tarps and canvas covers. It offers UV protection, provides total waterproofing against weather damage and stands up to temperatures as low as -50°F. Easily applied and removed, it can be simply recycled in the spring using Dr. Shrink's REBAG recycling system.

Southern anglers often use their boats all winter, but some don't. The same basic winterizing steps should be used for any boats stored for a length of time. In the case of wintertime southern angling, it's still important to protect the boat with a cover. It's also a good idea to use fuel stabilizer. I also like to keep my batteries continually charged with an inboard or portable trickle throughout the winter months. And, in areas where occasionally below freezing temperatures occur, again make sure all water from the bilge, lower unit and livewells is removed.

With proper storage, regardless of North or South, your boat will last longer, provide less hassle in running and continue to provide fun and relaxation.

Boat Storage Shed

Although your boat can be stored outside during the off season, in icy, winter weather, the best bet is inside storage. Even a duck boat used through the winter months should be stored inside. Otherwise you'll have frozen decoy bags, and an ice encrusted boat is just plain miserable and dangerous.

A simple open, lean-to shed attached to a garage or other building can be used as an open storage area. Or you may prefer to enclose the shed for more protection and security. The lean-to shown is easy to construct. It features a simple pole construction and metal roof. The roof is supported in a manner that sparrows and others birds can't perch above the boat and mess on it. The shed shown is designed as a drive-through building, open on both ends. I can pull my boat in place, even leave it attached to my truck between trips. Then I simply pull out the opposite end. Although the dimensions shown may not suit your space or needs, the general idea of

Storing your boat out of the weather, even in a simple shed, is better than outside storage. The shed shown is "drive-through" style. You can pull the boat under the shed, even leave hooked to your vehicle, then drive through for the next trip.

the shed can be customized to suit many different situations. The shed has a fairly shallow pitch and may not meet local building codes in some areas. Make sure you check with authorities. Or you can increase the pitch if it will fit your existing building and the ground slope near your building.

Materials

Qty.	Part	Dimensions
4	Poles	4 x 4" x 10'
6	Front headers	2 x 6" x 8'
2	Long end braces	2 x 4" x 15'
10	45° braces	2 x 6 x 36"
2	Building headers, cut to fit	2 x 6" x 12'
14	Rafter blocking, cut to fit	2 x 4" x 12'
15	Rafters	2 x 6" x 16'
2	End blocking, cut to fit	2 x 4" x 8'
2	Siding	4 x 8'
2	Fascia	$^{3}/_{4}$ x 6" x 12'
	Metal Roofing	16 x 24"

Boat Storage Shed cont'd

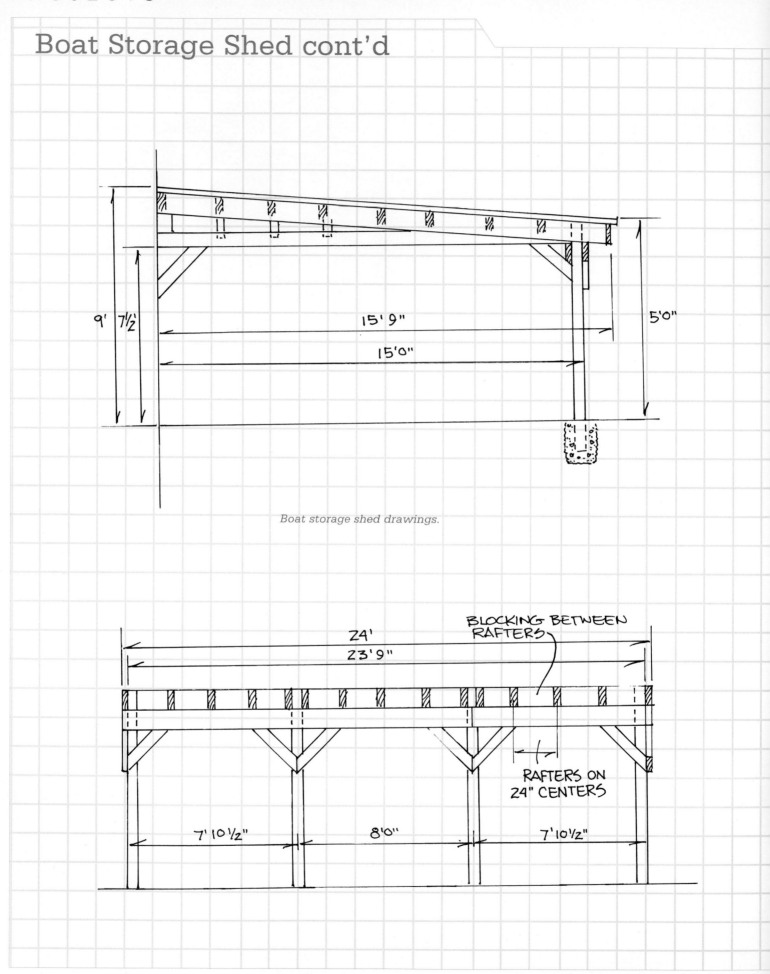

Boat storage shed drawings.

First step in construction is to lay out the pole locations. Measure for the outside corner poles and drive stakes at the rough locations. Note the corner posts should set in 1¾" to allow for the outside framing, plus the thickness of the existing building siding. Then use a tape measure diagonally from one corner of the existing building to the pole on the opposite corner. Measure the other corner pole location in the same manner. The measurements should be the same; if they are not, shift the stakes in or out until they are the same measurement. This creates a building square with the existing building. Drive stakes at the exact locations of the poles, including the other support poles.

Dig the holes for the support poles, making sure the holes extend below frost level in your area. Set the poles in place, again making sure they are located square with the existing building and plumb. Brace solidly with 2 x 4s attached to the poles and stakes driven into the ground. Pour concrete around the poles and allow to set up overnight.

Determine the height of the outside roof edge and attach the front 2 x 6 headers across the front of the outside posts. Attach the rear 2 x 6 headers across the back of the posts. Cut the post tops flush with the top edge of the header. Cut the 45° angle braces for the front and attach them to the posts and to the bottom of the header. Determine the height the top of the rafters will fall on the existing building. Attach a 2 x 6 header to the building to fasten the rafter ends in place. Determine the rafter spacing and attach metal rafter hangers for each rafter. These are fairly simple rafters, with no bird's mouth notch. But they must be cut at the proper angle to meet the house wall and at their outer ends. The simplest method is to lay a straight rafter (crown up) on top of both the header plate on the building and the one on the posts. Lay a straight edge against the inside of the header plate and against the rafter. Mark this angle to meet the wall header properly. Then measure the rafter length and mark the same angle on the outer end. Cut this

First step in construction is to locate the support posts and dig holes. Then set posts in place and plumb them.

Make sure all posts are well braced.

Boat Storage Shed cont'd

pattern rafter and make sure it fits properly to the house header and rests on the rafter hangers. If it fits, use it as a pattern to cut the remaining rafters. Cut the rafters to the correct angles and length. Then install all rafters, fastening them in the rafter hangers. The outer ends are toenailed into the post headers. 2 x 6 blocking is then fastened between the rafters over the front header to make them more secure, provide support and a nailing surface for the metal roof. Additional blocking is added between the rafters every 24" to provide additional support and nailing surfaces, toenailing one end of each block in place.

Cut and install the long 2 x 4 end braces. The best method of attaching to the existing building is with a block attached to the building the same manner as for the building header. Note the end brace on the building shown is tapered to meet the bottom of the rafter in order to gain height in the building. You may not need that height for your building and can keep the end brace full width. Then attach the end diagonal braces. These really aren't necessary but are a sort of decorative look to match the existing building design. You may need to install end blocking between the rafter and long end braces to provide a nailing surface for the siding. Notch the ends of the blocking so it comes out flush with the outer surfaces of the rafters and end braces. Attach siding to match the house to the ends and add trim as desired. A 2 x 6 fascia board is fastened over the ends of the rafters. Then attach the metal roofing material, allowing it to extend past the front siding by 2". You may prefer to utilize a plastic or fiberglass patio cover material instead of the metal. Paint to suit.

Add Quikrete around each post and allow to set up.

Fasten the header to the existing house wall; add joist hangers for the rafters.

Fasten the headers to the front support posts.

Cut rafters and fasten them to the front post headers . . .

. . . and down in the rafter hangers in the house header.

You can also organize existing storage compartments for specific items. Light clamps are available for holding stern and bow lights until needed. Paddle holders, battery trays and map pockets are all boat accessory items that can be used to organize storage compartments. You should also look for areas that are not used. One of the least used areas is the underside of compartment lids. Hook and loop strips can be glued to the underside of the lid. They can then hold landing nets, maps and other items you want to get to fairly quickly. The bilge area may also offer additional storage space, but the items should be placed in a waterproof box that is secured in position. Screen door handles can be glassed to the bottom of fiberglass boats and used with rubber shock cords to hold the box in place. These boxes are great for storing additional oil, work rags, even tools. Lure holders conveniently placed around the boat can be extremely useful. The simplest method of making a lure holder is to glue a foam block to the gunwale. Hook and loop strips glued and screwed to the inside of the gunwale on the side of the deck can be used to secure pork jars and scent jars, and even used as a drink holder.

Motor Storage Rack

Although many boats are stored with the motors on the boats, some smaller boats may be stored with the motor stored separately. This includes the smaller 10 horsepower and down sizes as well as transom mount trolling motors. A simple 2 x 4 rack can be fastened against a garage or shop wall and be used to hold trolling motors and small outboards securely in place.

If you store small motors off the boat when not in use, a simple 2 x 4 rack makes it easy to store them up off the garage floor.

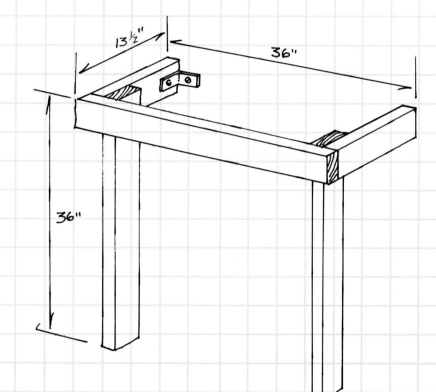

Motor storage rack drawing.

Materials

Qty.	Part	Dimensions
1	Front	2 x 4 x 36"
2	Sides	2 x 4 x 12"
2	Legs	2 x 4 x 36"

Battery Storage Tray

A battery should not be stored on a concrete floor as this will sap the energy from the battery. The simple rack shown not only holds the battery up off the floor or ground, but also provides a secure place to hold the battery charger as well.

A wooden tray will keep a battery off the floor, thus helping to maintain its charge.

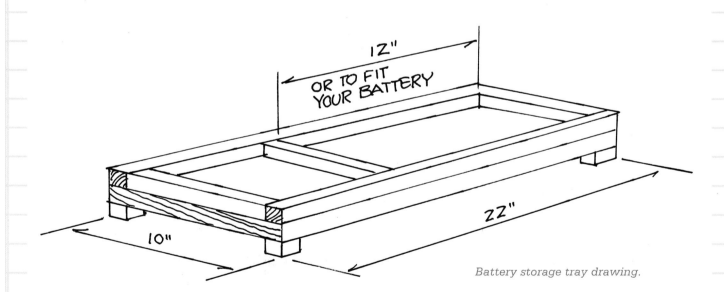

Battery storage tray drawing.

Materials

Qty.	Part	Dimensions
1	Bottom	$\frac{3}{4}$ x 10 x 22"
2	Sides	$\frac{3}{4}$ x $\frac{3}{4}$ x 22"
3	Ends and divider	$\frac{3}{4}$ x $\frac{3}{4}$ x $8\frac{1}{2}$"
4	Feet	$\frac{3}{4}$ x $\frac{3}{4}$ x $\frac{3}{4}$"

Boat Cleaning Storage Cabinet

Boat cleaning supplies and tools, extra oil for gasoline, ropes and other boating gear can easily be stowed in a wall-mounted cabinet in your garage or boathouse. The cabinet shown is a basic kitchen wall cabinet design. You can simply purchase a wall section from a local building supply dealer and mount it to your garage wall. Or build the cabinet shown. The cabinet is made of $3/4$" plywood with pine facers. It does not have a back but does have anchoring cleats inside and against the top and bottom. The doors are $3/4$" lip, using standard cabinet hardware.

First step is to cut the sides, bottom and top to width and length. Fasten the sides to the top. Then fasten the bottom to the sides. Note the bottom is set up 1/4" from the bottom edge of the sides. Fasten with glue and No. 6 finish nails set below the wood surface and filled with wood putty. Or use an air nailer brad driver. Cut the cleats and fasten to the inside top back and bottom pieces with self-starting wood screws. Cut the shelves and fasten in place with nails and glue. Or you can use shelf strips and hangers to create a more versatile interior.

Cut the top facer from 1x material to width and length. Fasten in place with glue and screws. Cut and fit the bottom facer in place. Note it runs from the top edge of the cabinet bottom to the bottom edges of the sides. Then cut and fit the side facers in place. There is no center facer on this cabinet.

Cut the doors to size. They meet in the middle and must be $3/8$" wider than one half the width of the opening. They must be $3/4$" longer than the door opening.

Boat cleaning and maintenance supplies can be kept on a simple wall shelf.

Materials

Qty.	Part	Dimensions
2	Sides, $3/4$" plywood	$11^{1}/_{4}$ x 36"
1 ea.	Top and bottom, $3/4$" plywood	$11^{1}/_{4}$ x $22^{1}/_{2}$"
2	Cleats	$3/4$ x 2 x $22^{1}/_{2}$"
1	Top facer	$3/4$ x 2 x 24"
1	Bottom facer	$3/4$ x 1 x 24"
2	Side facers	$3/4$ x 2 x 33"
2	Shelves	$3/4$ x $11^{1}/_{4}$ x $22^{1}/_{2}$"
2	Doors, $3/4$" plywood	$10^{3}/_{8}$ x $33^{3}/_{4}$"

Boat Cleaning Storage Cabinet cont'd

This allows you to create a $\frac{3}{8}$ x $\frac{3}{8}$" rabbet on the top, bottom and side edges of the doors for standard $\frac{3}{8}$" lip cabinet hardware. Make this rabbet with a straight bit in a router or by making two cuts on a table saw. Use a $\frac{1}{4}$" round-over bit in a router placed in a router table to slightly round the outside edges of the doors before

you cut the back rabbets. Hinge the doors in place and add magnetic catches inside to hold the doors shut. Then finish to suit and install knobs. Anchor to the wall with self-starting wood screws through the back cleats.

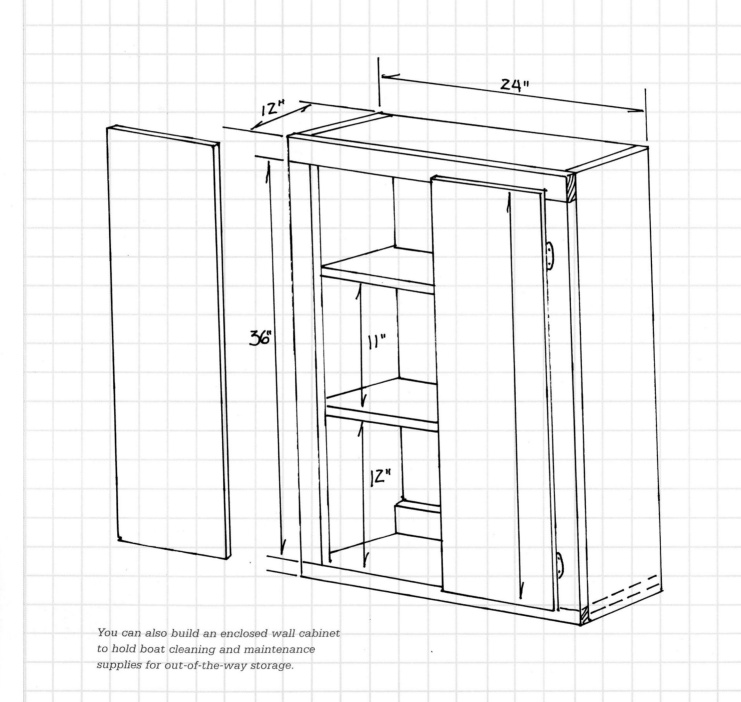

You can also build an enclosed wall cabinet to hold boat cleaning and maintenance supplies for out-of-the-way storage.

Rope Snag Rod

If you've ever tried to snag a loop of a rope around a tree stump, piling or other secure holder in wind or current, you'll appreciate the rope snag rod my nephew Morgan made for me. It's simply a 4' section of schedule 40 plastic plumbing pipe with an end cap glued on each end. Before gluing the end caps in place, bore a $\frac{3}{8}$" hole in their center. Bore a hold about 2" from one end of the pipe. Thread a rope through the hole and pull the rope out from the inside end of the pipe. Tie a secure knot in the rope end and pull it back so the knot is on the inside of the pipe. Then thread the rope through the hole of one end cap. Fish the rope down through the pipe and glue the cap in place. This creates a loop that can be pulled tight or opened for snagging the object. Thread the loose end of the rope through the opposite end cap and tie a knot in the end. Then glue that end cap in place. To use, open the loop, flip over the object and pull the loose end to tighten around the object. Then tie the loose end to the boat cleat. It's quick and easy.

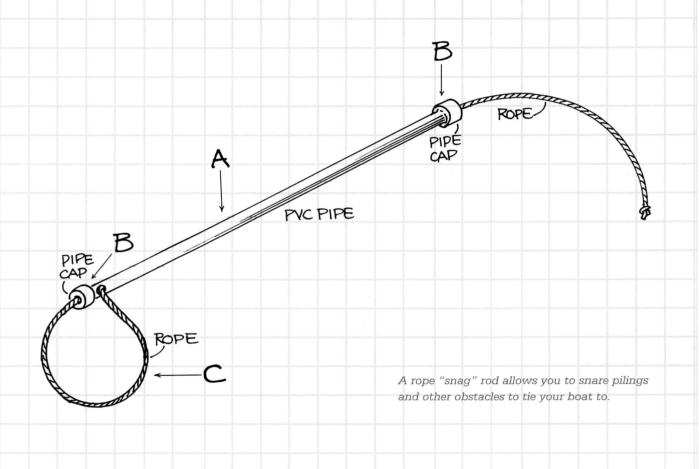

A rope "snag" rod allows you to snare pilings and other obstacles to tie your boat to.

Materials

	Qty.	Part	Dimensions
A	1	Handle	1" pvc x 36"
B	2	End caps	1" pvc caps
C	1	Rope	$\frac{3}{8}$ x 36"

Boating Chocks

A set of chocks can be invaluable in many boating situations. For instance, if you must park your boat on a sloping driveway or hillside, the trailer wheels should be chocked to prevent the trailer and boat from rolling downhill. When launching from steep and slick ramps, wheel chocks can also be used on your tow vehicle.

You can easily make a pair of chocks from a few parts. You'll need two pieces of 4 x 4 material, and it's best if they're of water resistant wood such as redwood or white cedar, or pressure-treated wood. The

blocks should be about 18" long and cut on each end at a 45° angle. Drill a hole in the center of the top of each block and install a screw eye. Then tie an 8" piece of polypropylene rope to the screw eyes.

To create more holding power on slick surfaces, cut strips of self-sticking tub or shower floor pieces and install on the bottoms of the chocks. You might also wish to paint them a bright orange or red color so you can find them quickly in a truck filled with gear.

Materials

	Qty.	Part	Dimensions
A	1	Chock	$3^1/_2$ x $3^1/_2$ x 18"
B	1	Screen-eye	$3/_8$ x $1^1/_2$"
C	1	Rope	$3/_8$ x 12"

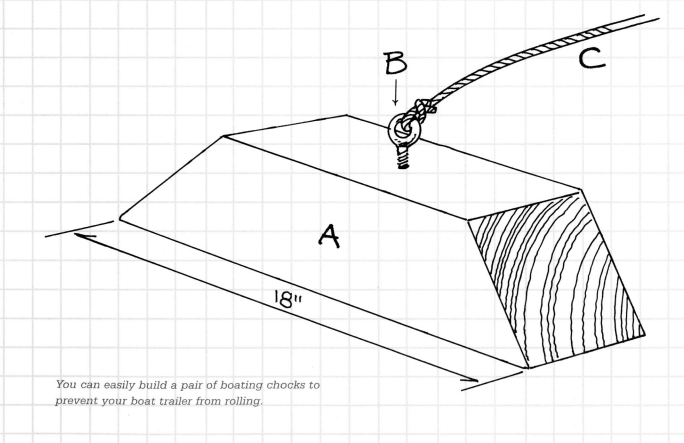

You can easily build a pair of boating chocks to prevent your boat trailer from rolling.

ATV STORAGE

ATVs and utility vehicles are built for tough use, and they can be stored outside. But inside storage not only lengthens their life, but also provides a safe, secure storage away from thieves.

The shed shown provides a secure lockable storage for your ATV with additional space for other items such as rack packs, gun scabbards, gasoline, tools and other accessories. One problem, however, had to be solved for the shed shown. The only location for the shed was on a slope. I could have constructed a wooden-floored shed, or used a concrete pad. In both cases, this would have added to the cost, and my desire was for an economical, easy-to-drive-into shed. The result is a "mini" pole-barn. Pole construction is one of the most economical methods of building construction, and it's also relatively easy.

An ATV storage shed can keep your valuable ATV locked up, safe and secure and out of the weather.

ATV Storage Shed

Basic construction consists of setting poles in holes in the ground and anchoring the poles in place with concrete. Pole barns are often made of round poles, but square posts can also be used, as in the shed shown. The poles or posts must be pressure treated or otherwise suitable for in-ground use. After the posts are set, girts, or horizontal nailing boards, are nailed to the posts and siding is anchored to the girts. Typically, a truss roof is then used to construct an open-type building. The small pole shed shown is also an excellent "practice" project for anyone wishing to construct a large pole building. The basic construction techniques shown can also be used to construct a larger building.

Before you begin construction, contact your local building authorities regarding any rules and regulations for pole buildings, as well as the recommended depth for the holes containing the poles. Also check for any standard rules, regulations and permits needed for constructing any building. The shed shown is permanent, not movable, so it may be subject to additional permits and regulations.

The first step is to lay out the building. Determine the direction of the building, aligning it with existing buildings as desired. Drive small stakes at each of the four corner locations as per the wall lengths, with the outside corners of the stakes the outside measurements of the poles. Note, this is not the final building size, as the 2 x 4 horizontals must also be figured in the final measurement. Measure diagonally from the outside edge of a stake corner to the opposite and then repeat for the other diagonal. These measurements should be the same to ensure a square building. If the measurements are not the same, shift the stakes until they are equal.

Dig the holes to the recommended depth. This may vary, but 2' would be considered adequate for this size building in most locations. Position the poles in place in the holes. On sloping lots, make sure the lower slope poles are not set so deep their tops are not high enough. Plumb the posts and brace them in place. Measure diagonally, inside to inside of the corner posts, and relocate them to reestablish a square building. Tack-nail a temporary girt to the posts and about a foot off the ground. This not only helps to maintain the correct distance between the posts, but also aligns the post sides. Locate the door posts and additional side posts and make sure they are the correct distance from the other posts as well as plumb. Brace them in place. Once all posts are

Materials

Qty.	Part	Dimensions
6	Treated posts	4 x 4" x 8'
2	Treated posts	4 x 4" x 10'
8	Lumber	2 x 4" x 12'
30	Lumber	2 x 4" x 8'
7	Wood siding	4 x 8'
6	Sheathing	1/2" x 4 x 8'
20	Treated lumber	1 x 6" x 8'
10 bags	60# concrete mix	
36	Truss plates	4 x 6"
18	Sheathing clips	
1 rl.	15# felt	
2 sq.	Asphalt or composite shingles	
5	Roof drip edge	
3 lbs.	Roofing nails	
3 lbs.	16 common nails	
3 lbs.	#4 galvanized nails	
8	Butt hinges and screws	4"
2	Padlock hasps	

properly located and braced, mix concrete and pour around the posts. Smooth the top of the concrete flush or slightly above ground level. Allow the concrete to cure for several days, and then remove the braces and temporary girts.

If on a sloping lot, position the lowest-to-ground level, bottom-side girt in place. Make sure it is level. Install the end girts, positioning them flush with the ends of the side girts and then positioning them level. Note, the girts are installed in place and the siding added, then the door openings cut out. Finally, install the next lower side girt. Once the bottom girts are in place, install the "skirting" boards of treated materials. On a sloping lot this may entail cutting some bottom edges of the skirting boards at an angle. Leave off the end skirt board until the siding is installed and doors are cut out.

Measure up from the bottom girts and mark the locations of the top side girts on each end post and the center side posts. Make sure the girts are level. A string level and line can be used for establishing these final pole heights, or you can use a girt, held in place and level, to mark the locations. Square around the posts and cut them to the correct height. Fasten the top side girts in place. These will protrude $1\frac{1}{2}$" past each post end. Then position a top side plate flush with the outside edges of the top girt and fasten it down on the top side girts and to the tops of the posts. Add the middle girts. Fasten a girt to the end starting at the top side girt and to the opposite corner post. Make sure it is level. Repeat for the opposite end. Then locate and position the middle end girts. Finally, position and anchor the opposite top side girt and the middle girt.

Measure the height needed for the over-the-door girt on the door posts. Make sure this is level and then cut each door post off to the correct height. Fasten the girt in place, then again nail a top plate down on each and flush with the outside edge of the girt. Repeat for the opposite end. Pole barns are typically braced with 45° angle braces anchored to each post and toe-nailed or screwed to the underside of the top girts. This creates the "wind-bracing" needed.

The next step is to build the trusses for the roof. Although construction is fairly simple, properly laying out the trusses and making the cuts at the proper an-gles is extremely important. Make a "try-fit" truss. Cut each piece to the correct size and angle. A radial arm or miter saw is excellent for this, as the angles can be set precisely. Or you can use a bevel square set to the proper angles and make the cuts with a portable circular saw. Lay the pieces on a flat, smooth surface and fasten together with metal truss plates or hardboard or plywood braces. Make sure the outside bottom corners are at 8'. Do not add the 2 x 4 braces at this time. Try-fit the sample truss on both ends as well as in the middle of the building. You'll need a helper for this chore. Adjust any angles or lengths as needed. Once you're satisfied with the fit, lay the sample truss on a smooth, flat surface. To speed up the process and provide more accurate truss construction, set up the saw and make all same-angle cuts. Then set up for the next angle and make all those cuts. Once all pieces are cut, position them down on the "master" truss and fasten together with truss plates on both sides, as well as with the 2 x 4 braces. Note the two end trusses do not have the 2 x 4 braces.

With a helper, erect one end truss and toe-nail it to the top plate. Use a 2 x 4 end brace temporarily nailed to the end girts and to the top corner of the truss, to hold the truss in place. Short blocks are nailed down on the top side plates and the trusses nailed into these blocks for additional strength. Position two more trusses in place, making sure they are located in the proper position. Then tack-nail a temporary 2 x 4 brace across their tops, again making sure they are positioned properly. Repeat for the opposite side. Then erect and install the remaining trusses, anchoring the end truss again with a temporary 2 x 4 brace to the end girts.

Now you're ready to install the siding. Position the end siding panels in place and anchor them solidly. Locate the corners of the door opening and the roof truss angles by boring small holes through the siding at the proper locations from the inside. Use a straight edge to mark between the holes. A portable circular saw, saber saw or even a reciprocating saw can then be used to cut off the excess plywood at the top ends and to make the door cut-outs. Once the door openings have been made, use 2 x 4 blocking flush with the outside edges of the posts, between

ATV Storage Shed cont'd

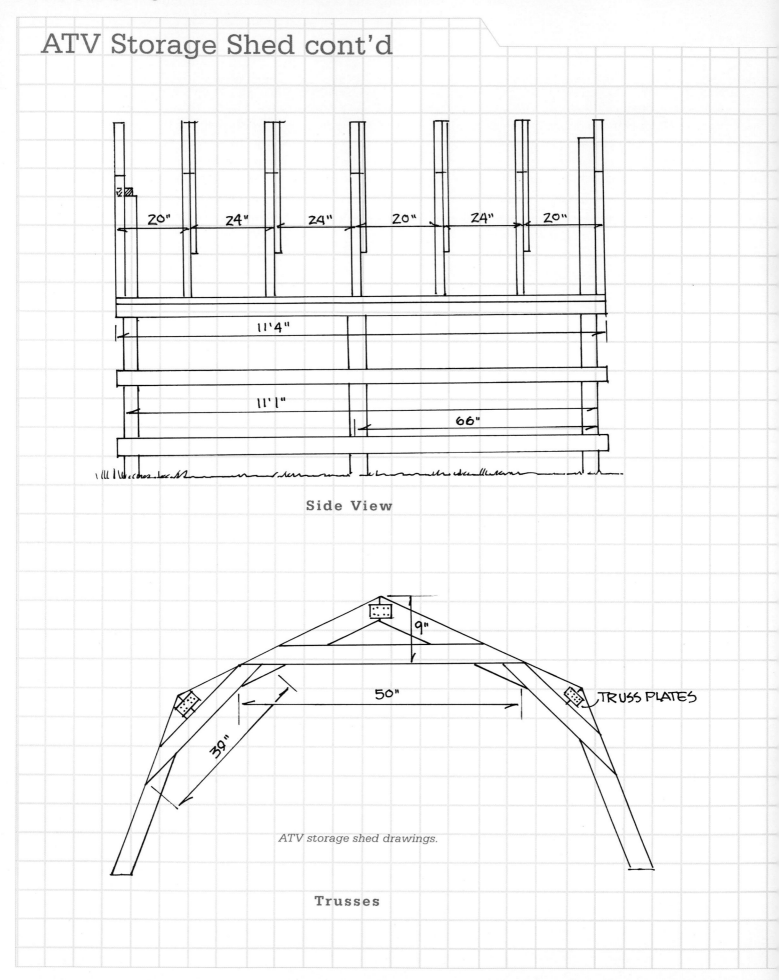

Side View

20" 24" 24" 20" 24" 20"

11'4"

11'1"

66"

9"

50"

39"

TRUSS PLATES

ATV storage shed drawings.

Trusses

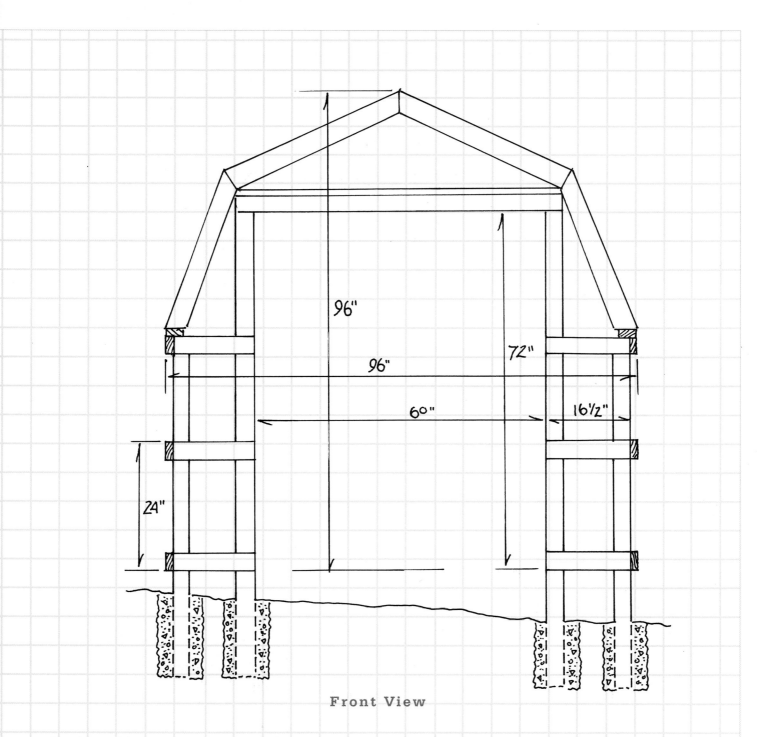

Front View

the girts and between the posts and the siding. Cut the siding for the sides and install it 1/2" lower than the top edge of the top side plates.

Install the roof sheathing on the lower roof sides, allowing it to protrude 4" over each end. Then cut and install the upper roof sheathings in place. Cut the end "hanging" rafters to the proper shape and size and fasten them to the protruding sheathing. Apply roofing felt and nail the asphalt shingles in place on the roof. Cut the trim to width and fasten on the corners,

at the roof edge and around the doors. Then add the "soffit."

Final construction step is to assemble the doors and hang them in place. The doors are constructed using the siding cut-outs from the ends. 2 x 2 backing is used for strength and 1 x 3 trim boards are added to the door fronts. The building can now be painted in traditional "barn-red" and white trim, or painted or stained any color pattern desired to match or complement existing buildings.

ATV Storage Shed cont'd

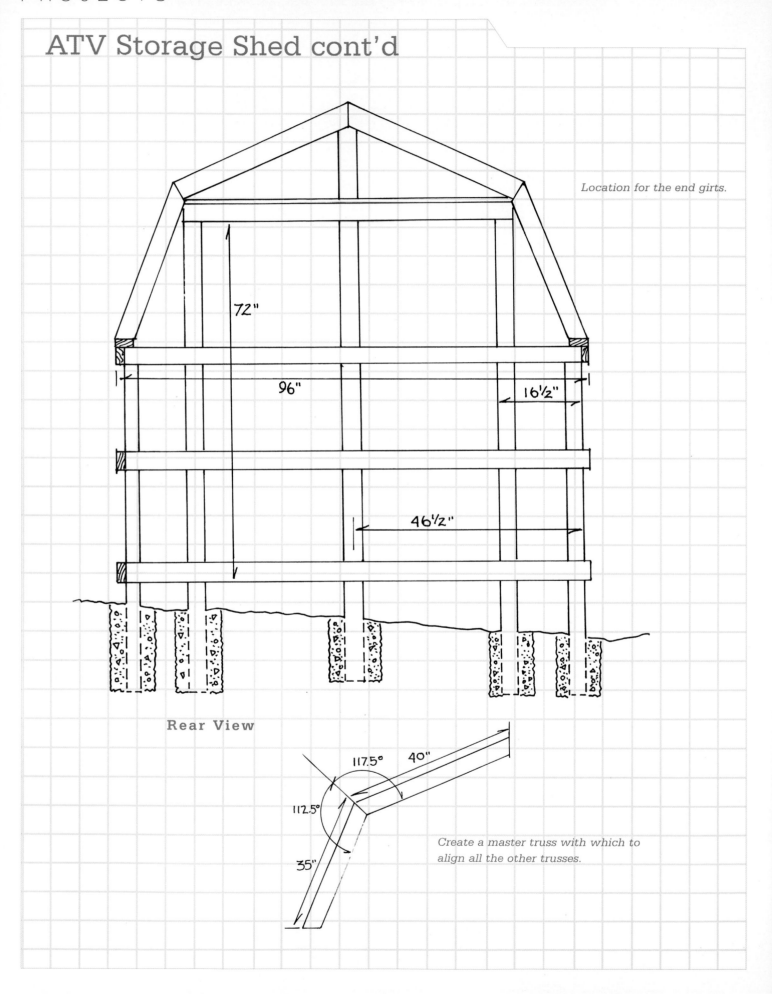

Location for the end girts.

72"

96"

16½"

46½"

Rear View

117.5°

40"

112.5°

35"

Create a master truss with which to align all the other trusses.

CAMPING GEAR

Camping gear can take up a lot of storage space, especially those that car, boat or canoe camp. Sleeping bags, coolers, tents, cook stoves, a food locker and cooking gear, in addition to just plain camping stuff, all require fairly large storage areas. Backpacking and hiking gear doesn't take up quite as much space, but is valuable equipment that must be stored properly. Shelves and large hook-style hangers can be used to loosely store stuff, but closable storage lockers will keep insects, mice and other pests out of sleeping bags and other gear.

Gear Cabinet

The cabinet shown not only suffices as a tight storage locker for tents and sleeping bags, but the top provides a work surface, or if preferred, a space to stack coolers, stoves and other gear. The cabinet is made of $3/4$" plywood with pine facers. Because the cabinet is made to hold some fairly heavy items, cleats support the bottom all around.

Gear Cabinet

First step is to cut the sides to size. Then use a router and a straight bit to rout a $\frac{1}{4}$ x $\frac{1}{4}$" rabbet in the inside back edges of the sides for a $\frac{1}{4}$" back. Cut the bottom piece to size, noting it is $\frac{1}{4}$" narrower than the side pieces. Stand one side piece on its front edge on a smooth flat surface such as a garage floor. You can hold this temporarily in place using a large wooden clamp. Position the bottom in place against the side. Note it fits 2" above the bottom edge of the side, and the front edge of the bottom is flush with the front edge of the side. Attach with glue and self-starting wood screws. Attach the opposite side piece in the same manner. Rip a back support strip and fasten it between the two sides at their top back corners, fitting the support strip behind the side rabbets. Cut the bottom cleats and attach them to the bottom front and back and to the two side pieces. Cut the back to size from $\frac{1}{4}$" plywood or particle board. Use a carpenter's square to assure the back is square, and then fasten the back in place with glue and cement-coated nails.

Turn the assembly over on its back. You may wish to have someone help lift it up on a pair of low sawhorses. Cut and install the divider. Note the cabinet is divided into two sections, with one section smaller to hold sleeping bags and the other longer for holding items such as tents. Cut the divider from plywood and install in place. Make sure it is installed square with the rest of the cabinet. Cut the bottom facer board and fasten it over the sides, the bottom and bottom front cleat. Use self-starting wood screws, or finish nails driven below the wood surface and the holes filled with wood putty. Install the top facer board in the same manner. Then install the side facers. Finally install the divider facer and the other horizontal facer. The divider facer is fastened down over the divider. The second horizontal facer is installed with glue blocks behind it to help secure it in place.

Cut the doors to size and shape, making sure they fit properly in the openings. Hinge in place with exposed hinges and add knobs and magnetic catches to hold the doors closed. The top shown is also $\frac{3}{4}$" plywood, with a $\frac{1}{4}$" hardboard surface for a smoother surface. You could also utilize a plastic laminate top if you prefer a cleanable work surface. Regardless, cut the top to size and shape. The top is held in place with cleats fastened to the inside edges of the sides, back support board and front facer. Fasten these in place with screws. Then drive screws up through the cleats into the top, making sure the screws don't protrude through the top.

Sand the entire cabinet smooth and add the finish of your choice.

Materials

Qty.	Part	Dimensions
2	Sides, $\frac{3}{4}$" plywood	$23\frac{1}{4}$ x 36"
1	Bottom, $\frac{3}{4}$" plywood	23 x $58\frac{1}{2}$"
1	Bottom cleat, back	$\frac{3}{4}$ x $1\frac{1}{4}$ x $58\frac{1}{2}$"
1	Bottom cleat, front	$\frac{3}{4}$ x $1\frac{1}{4}$ x $58\frac{1}{2}$"
1	Interior divider cleat	$\frac{3}{4}$ x $1\frac{1}{4}$ x 23"
1	Interior divider, $\frac{3}{4}$" plywood	23 x 34"
1	Back support strip	$\frac{3}{4}$ x 4 x $58\frac{1}{2}$"
1	Back, $\frac{1}{4}$" plywood	34 x $59\frac{1}{2}$"
1	Top facer	$\frac{3}{4}$ x 2 x 60"
1	Bottom facer	$\frac{3}{4}$ x 2 x 60"
4	Vertical facers	$\frac{3}{4}$ x 2 x 32"
3	Top support cleats, cut to fit	$\frac{3}{4}$ x 2 x 23"
1	Top, $\frac{3}{4}$" plywood	24 x 60"
3	Doors, $\frac{3}{4}$" plywood	$17\frac{1}{4}$ x $31\frac{1}{4}$"
3 pr.	Hinges	
3	Knobs	
3	Magnetic catches	

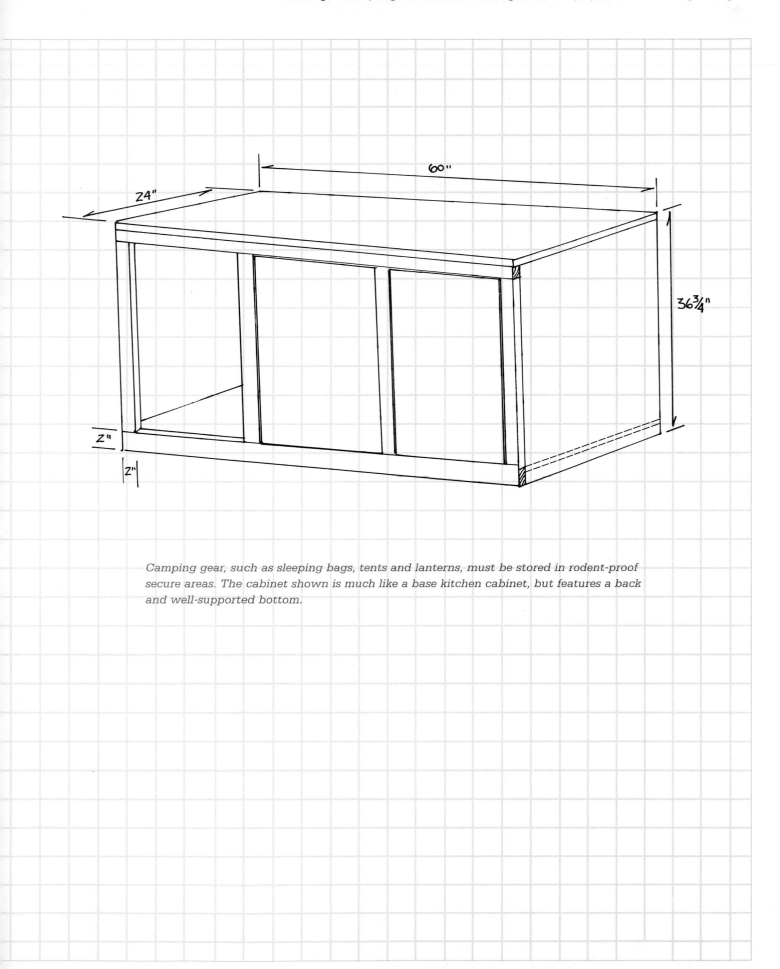

Camping gear, such as sleeping bags, tents and lanterns, must be stored in rodent-proof secure areas. The cabinet shown is much like a base kitchen cabinet, but features a back and well-supported bottom.

Grub Box

Camp cookery, eating utensils and the basic cooking needs such as flour, oil, salt, pepper and so forth are best organized into a grub box. Not only does this organize the gear at camp site, but it provides a means of keeping the items protected at camp, as well as storing them safely and securely at home. The box should be sized to fit your needs; for instance, an automobile grub box must be sized to fit your automobile, whether a car trunk, SUV or pickup bed. But don't make the box so big and bulky you can't readily lift it in and out for transportation. I did that several years ago. Not only was the box big, bulky and heavy, but it was hard to reach items in the back. The box shown, however, is fairly easy to handle and keeps all the necessary items. The box is assembled from $\frac{1}{2}$" plywood, using cleats glued in all corners for extra strength. Cut the top, bottom, sides and back from plywood. Fasten all pieces together with self-starting wood screws and glue in the glue blocks. Cut the dividers to size and shape from $\frac{1}{4}$" plywood and glue them in place. Then cut the front drop-down door and hinge it in place. Locate a hasp on the top to hold the door closed. Finish to suit.

If you camp by automobile, or wagon train, a grub box can help organize cooking gear and cooking necessities.

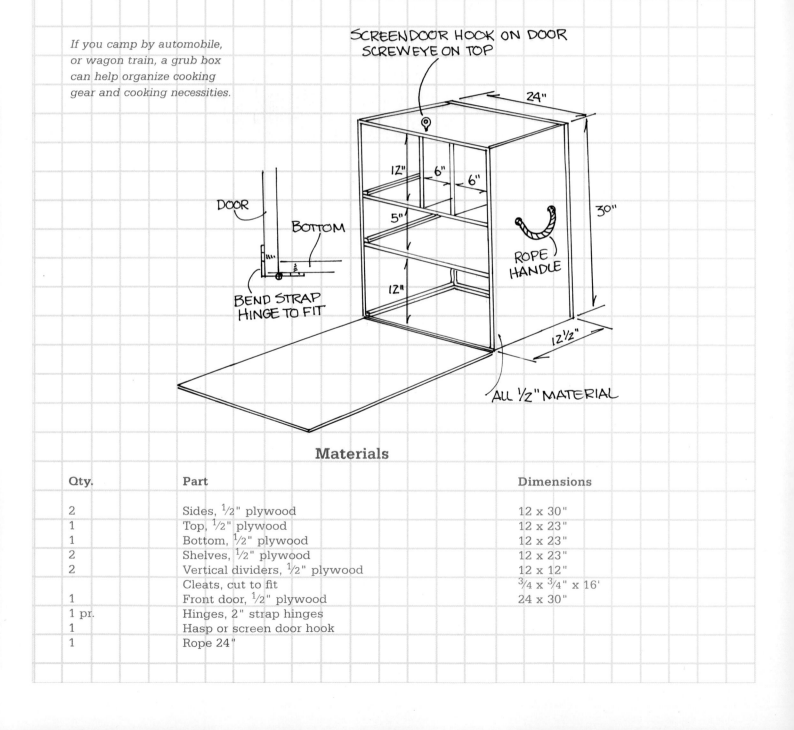

Materials

Qty.	Part	Dimensions
2	Sides, $\frac{1}{2}$" plywood	12 x 30"
1	Top, $\frac{1}{2}$" plywood	12 x 23"
1	Bottom, $\frac{1}{2}$" plywood	12 x 23"
2	Shelves, $\frac{1}{2}$" plywood	12 x 23"
2	Vertical dividers, $\frac{1}{2}$" plywood	12 x 12"
	Cleats, cut to fit	$\frac{3}{4}$ x $\frac{3}{4}$" x 16'
1	Front door, $\frac{1}{2}$" plywood	24 x 30"
1 pr.	Hinges, 2" strap hinges	
1	Hasp or screen door hook	
1	Rope 24"	

Camp Lantern Box

One of the most fragile camping items is a camp lantern. You can, however, easily assemble a box to protect the lantern during transport and storage. The box is made of $\frac{3}{8}$" plywood, glued together with blocks. Cut all pieces to size and assemble with glue and self-starting wood screws into the blocks. Cut the top piece to size and fasten it in place with hinges and a hasp. Add the handle. Paint or stain to suit. Adding a piece of foam around the lantern in the box adds to the protection.

A simple wooden lantern box can protect your camping lantern from breakage.

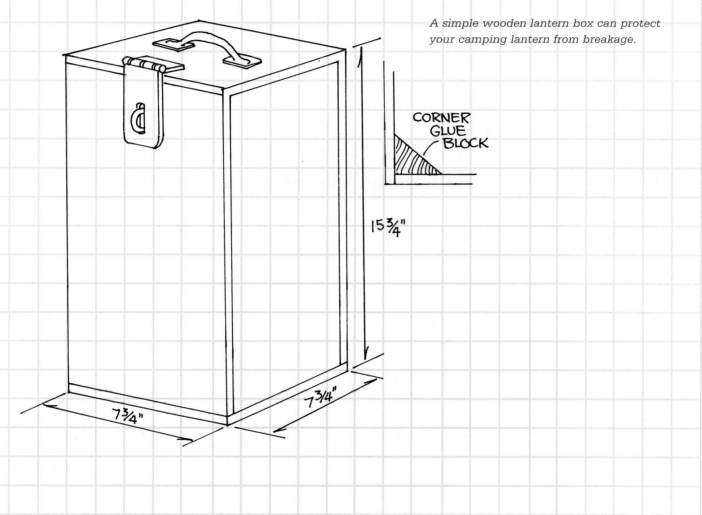

15¾"

CORNER GLUE BLOCK

7¾"

7¾"

Materials

Qty.	Part	Dimensions
2	Sides, $\frac{3}{8}$" plywood	7 x 15"
1	Front, $\frac{3}{8}$" plywood	7¾ x 15"
1	Back, $\frac{3}{8}$" plywood	7¾ x 15"
1	Bottom, $\frac{3}{8}$" plywood	7¾ x 7¾"
1	Top, $\frac{3}{8}$" plywood	7¾ x 7¾"
4	Glue blocks	¾ x ¾ x 15"
2	Hinges	
1	Hasp	
1	Handle	

MAINTENANCE TOOLS

Maintaining boats, ATVs and trailers is basic mechanics work, and requires a working space, workbench and mechanics tools. A garage or separate shop can provide comfortable, out-of-the-weather working space. I did, however, once build a fiberglass bass boat under a shade tree in our yard. A good solid workbench with a good solid vise is a necessity.

For boat motor work and some ATV work you'll need both metric and standard mechanics tools. The wrench set should include the most popular sizes in combination box-open end and also socket sets. Craftsman offers a 79-piece Marine Boat Repair tool set, and both an import and domestic motorcycle (ATV) tool set. You'll also

Working on boats, ATVs and camping gear can not only be a pleasant off-season chore, but can help your gear to last longer and work better and safer.

need a torque wrench. A selection of screwdrivers and pliers are necessary. A tape measure and hammers, both woodworking and ball-peen, are needed. A floor jack for lifting trailers for tire and bearing work is a necessity for this type of work. Craftsman also sells a floor jack made just for ATVs and it allows you to lift the entire vehicle off the ground. If you intend to do any engine installation you'll need a chain hoist or other heavy-duty lifting tool. An air compressor and air tools are also a must, not only for airing up tires, but wrenches, sanders, spray guns and dust blowers can also be helpful for the serious boat rigger and tinkerer. A shop vac can be used to clean up the boat, as well as vacuum away fiberglass and aluminum dust and pieces where you've been rigging or adding gear.

A lot of boat and ATV repair and maintenance consists of electrical chores.

A roll-around tool cart can hold tools and provide a workspace.

You'll need an electrical crimping and stripping tool, a solder gun, a battery load tester, and a multi-meter for testing. And, of course, you'll also need a battery charger.

A few specialty tools are needed for boats. A prop wrench and a piece of 2 x 4 are needed to remove props, although a sturdy socket set with a long handle can also be used. Running wires or cables through a fully assembled boat requires a rigging wire. This is simply a piece of stiff wire, such as No. 9 wire, that can be pushed and threaded through the compartments and rigging tubes. The electrical wire is then attached to the end of the rigging wire with electrician's tape and pulled through. Actually, a coat hanger straightened out can be used for short pulls. You'll also need a

A good set of standard and metric wrenches are necessary.

motor flush bonnet. This attaches to a garden hose and fits over the water intake of the motor. This allows you to run the engine without having it submersed in water for testing or repair.

A cordless electric drill/driver is one of the handiest of tools. They can be used for drilling holes and driving screws. And, these days a wide variety of models are available. You may also wish to consider an impact driver for serious driving chores.

Fiberglass boats and the plastic fenders and other parts of ATVs can become dulled and scratched over time. A power buffer can make quick work of bringing them back to their original shine. A cordless buffer/polisher makes it easy to work on boat hulls in out-of-the-way places.

An impact driver can save a lot of hard work.

The Craftsman ATV jack makes it easy to work on your ATV, change tires, work on brakes, etc.

An electrical tester and tools are necessities, and, far right, you'll need an air compressor.

A sturdy workbench is a must.

Portable shop lights provide light where and when you need it.

A welder can be extremely handy for many chores.

CHAPTER 6

Dressing, Butchering, Skinning, and Tanning

One of the main purposes of hunting or fishing for many of us is obtaining food, as well as furs, antlers and other part of the wild game and fish we pursue. Many a deer, elk and even small game has been skinned and dressed hanging from a handy tree limb in the backyard. For many years an old oak near our back door provided just the right limb for the purpose. And, the quartered game was butchered on our back porch. Over the years, however, we've found a dedicated work space for these chores not only makes it easier, but also provides better storage for tools and gear.

WORK SPACE

A corner of a garage, a small separate shed or even a portion of a barn or other outbuilding can provide a good work space. Actually the work space for the most part should be unheated as meat should be kept cold during the butchering process. The main objective is to have a place out of the weather because invariably, the winter months can provide lots of cold rain, snow and other weather. You may prefer both an outside and inside work area. The outside area can be used for hanging and skinning deer and big game. The inside area then becomes the butchering area. A shade over a fish-dressing table can be mightily appreciated during the hot summer months as well.

You'll also need a solid working table. Ideally, it should be at a comfortable "work" height for your stature. The table top should also be easily cleanable. A plastic laminate top is a good choice, although in the past we've simply used plastic tablecloths for covering wooden tables for butchering. Large cutting boards are placed on the table top for the actually cutting of meat. These can be purchased cutting boards, or discarded plastic laminate sink cut-outs. Several years ago we were able to purchase a couple of stainless steel commercial kitchen tables at an auction.

Many a critter has been skinned and butchered hanging from a handy tree limb.

They are extremely easy to clean and maintain, although we don't do any actual cutting on the surfaces, but again utilize cutting boards over their tops.

In the absence of a sturdy tree limb, you'll need a meat pole. We have one constructed outside for use in good weather. A pair of tall Osage orange posts are sunk in concrete with a cross beam between them. These Osage orange (hedge) posts will last for many years. You might prefer to construct a meat pole of pressure-treated 2 x 6s, mounted on sturdy treated posts, also set in concrete. During inclement weather we utilize a sturdy beam in our barn for hanging meat, skinning and quartering deer and other game.

I've used an ATV to pull deer up on the meat pole, but a sturdy game hoist is the best bet. An alternative is an electric winch fitted solidly in place. In addition to

A work space set aside for skinning and butchering chores makes for easier clean-up, providing better working conditions. It may be inside or out.

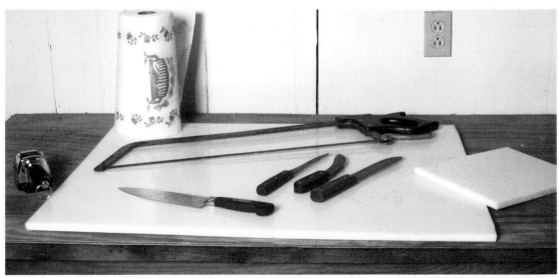

the meat pole you'll also need gambrels for hanging the carcasses. These should be sized to the game you're dressing or skinning. Purchased gambrels are available, but they're easily constructed if you have a welder and simple welding skills.

It's important to keep game carcasses cool, chilling them down as quickly as possible. Deer and some big game meat should also be aged by hanging. If the temperature stays in the low 40s, this can be done in the open. In warm weather, or if you live in the South or Southwest, this isn't often possible. In mid Missouri where we live, invariably the week of gun deer season turns off hot, often in the 60s and 70s. For several years we skinned and quartered deer as quickly as possible, then placed the quarters in an old refrigerator to chill and age for about a week. A few years back we purchased an

A sturdy meat pole is a necessity.

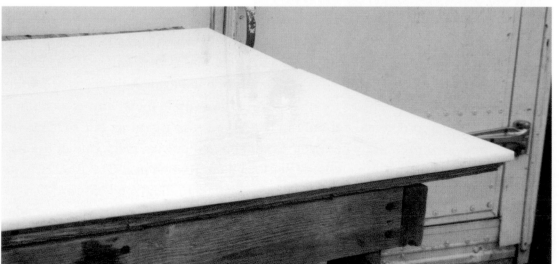

A sturdy worktable with a cleanable surface is important. The latter can be purchased, easy-to-clean cutting boards.

In some parts of the country you may need some sort of refrigeration to cool down the meat. We purchased the body of an old refrigeration truck at a reasonable price.

old refrigerator truck bed. It works great for the chore. There are, however, small commercial units that can also be purchased. Or, you can make your own "walk-in" cooler. This consists of a tightly enclosed box, preferably inside or in the shade. The box should be constructed of 2 x 6 framing utilizing 36 factor or greater insulation to provide adequate insulation. The door, floor and roof must be insulated as well. A small refrigeration unit can then be used to keep the meat cool.

Knives and Other Butchering Gear

Regardless of whether skinning and dressing fish, big game, small game or game birds, you just can't have enough knives. Depending on your favorite species, you'll need small pocket knives for small game and game birds, fillet knives for fish, skinning knives for small and big game and all kinds of butchering knives. It's important to purchase good quality knives for these chores. Low-grade metal knives won't hold an edge and cause problems, not only in continued resharpening, but causing you to apply unneeded pressure where you might slip and cut yourself. One of the best tactics is to purchase a complete knife set for butchering chores. The Chef'sChoice Trizo Professional 10X cutlery set utilizes space-age technology and old-world craftsmanship resulting in a unique Trizo stainless steel, a technologically advanced alloy containing twice the carbon and ten times the molybdenum. It is so tough it is guaranteed an ultra sharp edge that stays sharper up to ten times longer than any other kitchen knife in the world. We've used the Chef'sChoice cutlery for several years and can highly recommend them.

In addition to knives a pair of game shears, such as those from Chef'sChoice, can be invaluable. A hand-meat saw is necessary for quartering big game, as well as for making cuts such as for chops and ribs. You may prefer a hatchet for splitting rib cages and pelvic bones. A variety of field-dressing saws are available for these chores as well. You'll also need lots of plastic, easily cleaned tubs and pans and soft clean rags for wiping surfaces and cleaning your hands. You should always wear disposable protective gloves when field dressing or dressing any game. The fur and feathers of game animals and birds can harbor ticks and disease pathogens.

A meat grinder is necessary for producing ground meat from game animals, and even birds. Incidentally, ground goose and duck meat makes great tasting summer sausage. These grinders can be hand cranked or electric. If electric, purchase a heavy-duty model that will handle the tougher game meats. VillaWare carries three models of electric meat grinders that feature stainless steel cutting blades, cutting disks, feeding screws and tubes that are durable as well as corrosion resistant. These include the Power Grinder, ProGrinder and Elite ProGrinder.

You'll need lots of knives, skinning, butohering, small and large. We've found the Chef'sChoice Trizo Professional 10X knives some of the best for butchering. A number of excellent skinning knives are available, including those from Katz.

A meat grinder can be used to make sausage, burger and for ground jerky. The VillaWare models are an excellent choice.

A meat slicer is also an extremely important tool for many butchering chores. Because of cross-contamination and disease concerns, most butchers will no longer assist hunters in slicing their freshly caught game and wildfowl. We tested a number of excellent Chef'sChoice slicer models from EdgeCraft. Their extensive line of electric food slicers are the perfect solution for outdoor enthusiasts who want to slice their own game, make homemade jerky or slice a wide variety of foods including vegetables, breads and cheese. For instance, their heavy-duty Model 645, Professional VariTilt commercial-quality slicer offers heavy-duty rugged aluminum and stainless steel construction, true gravity feed (30° incline) and precision thickness control. The powerful commercial-grade condenser motor insures continuous, efficient, smooth and whisper-quiet gear drive operation.

The Model 668 slicer features a fully hardened commercial-quality fine-edge surgical stainless steel blade and blade cover to reduce friction during slicing. An interlock system disables operation of the slicer and blocks access to the blade edge when the food carriage is removed from the unit. Rubber feet provide excellent stability and hold the unit securely to the work surface. The slicer's cantilever design makes food preparation and clean-up effortless. The design allows for easy access to

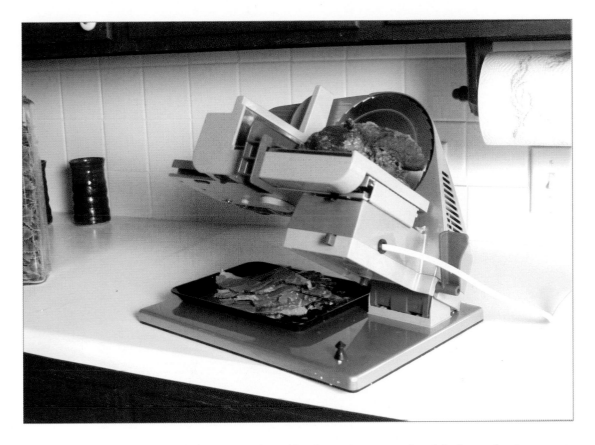

The Chef'sChoice 645, Professional VariTilt meat slicer makes quick work of any slicing chore, is easy to use and easy to clean.

all parts of the slicer and the base plate, food carriage, cutting blade and other parts also remove easily for cleaning.

If you intend to butcher and process deer and big game meat in the traditional cuts, an electric meat band saw can be mighty handy. A number of these have become available including one from Bass Pro and Grizzly. Both feature a stainless steel sliding table, easy clean-up and also a meat grinder and sausage stuffer.

Fish Cookers

A platter of sizzling crappie fillets is the end result of many crappie trips. The culinary result or tastiness to most of us crappie aficionados, however, depends on many factors, not the least, the method of cooking. Deep-frying is one of the most effective methods because the meat is cooked so rapidly the juices are sealed in and there is less cooking oil soaked up, resulting in "cleaner tasting" and more healthful fillets. Crappie fillets can be deep-fried in a big skillet on a stove, and yes they taste great fried fresh from the water on the shore, along with a pan of fried potatoes. A propane fish cooker, however, makes the chore much easier and faster.

Over the years I've tested a number of fish cookers. I know, tough job! But I have accumulated some ideas on what suits my cooking style best. Yours, however, may be different. Fish cookers consist of a burner unit, with or without legs, and a pot to hold the fish. Some may also include baskets—easy for lifting out cooked fillets—and a lid,

Fish cookers make it easy to fry a batch of fillets, even for a crowd, while larger turkey fryers can be used for popular Cajun-style wild turkey.

although the latter is not used for the actual cooking of crappie. A basic cooker can be used for deep-frying, boiling or even pan frying. Any number of deep-fryers is available including several from Bass Pro. Stainless steel, aluminum and cast-iron cooking pots are available. Stainless steel cleans up easier, but it's harder to keep the temperature regulated if cooking for some time or for a crowd. Aluminum cleans up easy and holds the heat fairly well. Cookers may feature a lift-out basket with a handle or bail. Our church has a huge fish-fry each year and we cook several hundred pounds of fish. We've found the easiest method of cooking those amounts is to use a skimmer to lift out the individual pieces of fish as they fry rather than lifting out the baskets, which causes more mess.

Turkey Fryers

Similar in use, but simply with a deeper pot and a rack and lifting handle, is a turkey deep-fryer. These pots allow you to deep-fry a whole turkey Cajun style. They have become increasingly popular in past years, and do a good job on wild turkey, which is less moist than domestic turkey meat. With an additional pot used for purposes other than cooking with oil, your fish cooker or turkey fryer can also make delicious gumbo or soup in volume, or boil shrimp, lobster and crabs as well.

Fish Cleaning Workplace and Tools

I've dressed fish with my pocketknife at the river's edge and filleted a cooler full of panfish at a marina fish table. Fish should be dressed as soon as possible after they are caught, or kept iced or alive and well until they can be dressed. One friend of mine who owns a fairly large lake and manages it for big bass has his own slot limit and culls bass in that size. He carries a battery-powered fillet knife in his boat and the culls are rapped on the head with a club, immediately dressed and put on ice in plastic bags. A huge, soft-shelled turtle lives in the lake and follows his johnboat around like a puppy dog waiting for a treat—and he is well fed. Make sure you understand fish and game laws concerning keeping fish intact for transportation.

For most of us fish dressing takes place back at home. I've cleaned many a fish in the kitchen sink, late at night after a long drive from a successful fishing trip. At

Fish cleaning can be as simple as a pocketknife at streamside.

The Bass Pro Pro-Fillet
Cleaning System features an
over-sized sink with sinkhole
for waste.

The Bass Pro Bucket Board
fish cleaning system can be
used at camp, or even in a
boat, placed over a plastic
bucket.

A permanent fish cleaning station, out of the kitchen, is best for those who clean a lot of fish.

best it's a messy chore. The solution is a fish cleaning station or workplace. Portable fish cleaning stations are available that can be taken to camp with you or used at home. The Pro-Fillet Cleaning System from Bass Pro features an oversized sink with a raised, non-slip cleaning surface with ruler and slotted knife storage, recessed side drains and a built-in slot for 2 x 4 legs (not included). The Pro-Fillet comes with a fillet clamp, sinkhole waste bag clamp, side fillet bag clamp, plus three waste and three fillet storage bags. You can place the unit on a picnic table or add the legs for easy free-standing use. One of the simplest cleaning stations is the Bass Pro Bucket Board. You can even use this on your boat. The board is a lightweight, high density polyethylene board that is easily cleaned, and fits snugly onto any 2, 4, 5 or 6 gallon bucket (not included). The board includes knife storage and a permanent 17" ruler.

My fish cleaning station is a permanent outside work area. It begins with an old commercial, stainless steel table purchased at an auction, placed on a concrete pad next to the back side of my garage. Above the table is an electrical outlet protected by a ground-fault interrupter. Because I often clean fish at night, after a full day of fishing, I've installed a light with a photocell over the work area. When I step up to the work table the light switches on. I've installed a faucet with a short piece of hose next to the table for easy clean-up.

Storage Cabinet

This small, weather-resistant storage cabinet holds fillet knives, plastic bags and other fish cleaning supplies. The storage cabinet is very simple, made of water-resistant white cedar and with a lip around the outside to keep out rainwater. Cut the top, bottom and sides to length from a cedar 1 x 8 and fasten with glue and exterior wood screws. Cut the support cleats and install inside, one to the bottom and one to the top.

Glue up the door front from cedar stock with exterior glue and cut to size. Rip the lip pieces to width, cut their edges to a 45° miter joint and add to the inside of the door front with glue and screws. Rip the cabinet lip pieces and joint them with 45° miter corners around the outside edge of the cabinet. Hinge the door and add a magnetic catch on the inside to hold the door shut.

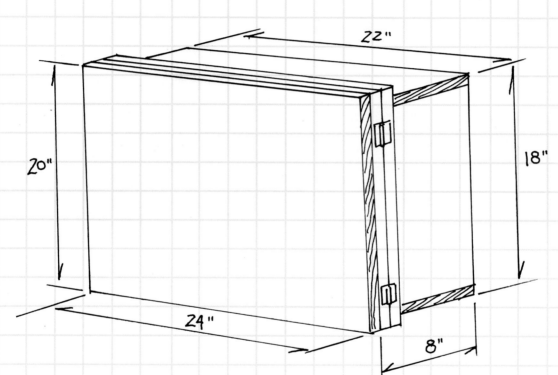

A weather-proof cabinet can be used to hold fish cleaning supplies.

Materials

Qty.	Part	Dimensions
1 ea.	Top and bottom	$3/4$ x 8 x 22"
2	Sides	$3/4$ x 8 x $16^{1}/2$"
2	Support cleats	$3/4$ x $1^{1}/2$ x $20^{1}/2$"
1	Door front	$3/4$ x 24 x 20"
2	Side, door lip pieces	$3/4$ x $3/4$ x 20"
2	Top and bottom, door lip pieces	$3/4$ x $3/4$ x 24"
2	Side cabinet lip pieces	$3/4$ x $3/4$ x 20"
2	Bottom and top cabinet lip pieces	$3/4$ x $3/4$ x 24"
1 pr.	Hinge	
1	Screen door latch or magnetic catch	

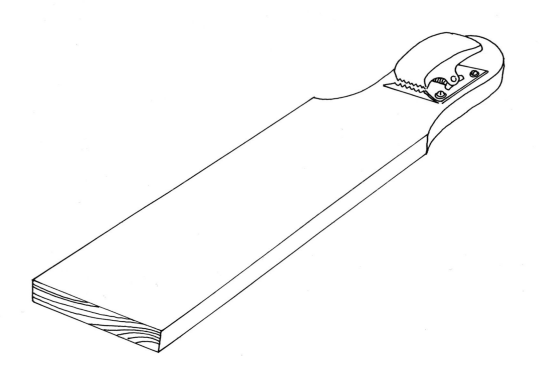

Fish-cleaning boards, such as the Original Clean-A-Fish fillet board, make it easy to hold slippery fish while cleaning them.

Fish Fillet Board

In addition to the work table, I also have easily cleaned cutting boards as the stainless steel table top is hard on knives. Regardless of what you use for cutting surfaces, they must be easily cleaned. One of the most common is the Original Clean-A-Fish fillet board, from Intruder. It's been around for several decades and features a sturdy, fine-grained hardwood that won't dull knives, yet cleans up easily. Mounted to the board is a strong-jawed steel fillet clamp featuring sharp V-grooves that hold fish securely while leaving both hands free for the cleaning chores. Or you can purchase the Intruder clamp to mount to your own board. You can also make up your own wood cutting board, but it should be of a hard, smooth wood such as maple for easy clean-up. A number of synthetic cutting boards are also available.

Fillet Knives

Knives are a necessity of course, and fish filleting knives are the best choice. These are available in a wide range of shapes, sizes and materials. Quality can vary quite a bit as well. It's extremely important to purchase only good-quality fillet knives. The blades of the better fillet knives are made of rust-resistant, high-carbon stainless steel. Fillet knives are also available with straight or serrated edge blades. Straight-edge blades are fine for panfish, but the serrated edges work better on

A wide range of fillet knives are available in all sizes. Make sure you purchase a good brand knife.

larger fish, or those that require cutting through heavy scales. Kershaw has an excellent fillet knife that comes with two removable blades, a straight and a serrated edge blade.

Fillet knife blades are also available in several lengths. If you normally fillet small and pan-sized fish, the shorter blades of 6" are perfect and they are not as awkward to carry on your belt. Knives are available with blades up to 12" in length. Also available from Kershaw is their seven-step adjustable fillet knife. This allows you to adjust the blade length as needed. Fillet knives are also available with either traditional wooden or molded soft-grip handles. One of the best I've tested is the Katz fillet knife. Many fillet knives come with a sheath, which may be leather, Cordura or molded plastic. The latter, such as the sheath with the Katz knife, has become increasingly popular. Steaking and planking larger fish also requires larger butcher knives and cleavers.

If you clean a large number of fish such as crappie, catfish or panfish, you'll find nothing beats an electric fillet knife for filleting. I've had a Mister Twister version for many years and I really don't know how many fish it has dressed. It is available either as a 110-volt or 12-volt battery powered model that can be used at camp, or in a boat. The American Angler fillet knife, with its pointed blades, is a great choice for saltwater anglers. These days a number of cordless rechargeable fillet knives area available, including the Rapala model.

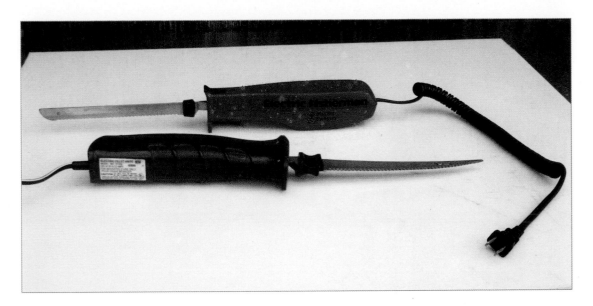

An electric fillet knife makes even a cooler full of panfish easy to clean. The Rapala cordless model can be used anywhere.

Other Gear

Fish fillet gloves can protect your hands not only from sharp knives, but also the sharp gill plates of fish such as walleye and white bass. Intruder Stainless Steel Fillet Gloves feature a stainless steel core for strength and cut resistance with a high-tech wrapping of interwoven polyester and vinyl material for comfort, resistance to stains and odors and easy washing. The FDA/USDA-approved materials meet rigid food service industry standards. Other fish cleaning tools include scalers for those who prefer to scale panfish. For skinning fish such as catfish, you'll need a pair of fish-cleaning pliers. Bass Pro has two models, including their Deluxe Fish Skinning pliers that have a sturdy grip and vinyl-coated handles for comfort.

Make a "Priest"

In days past, a short sturdy club was traditionally used by fishermen to give a sharp blow to the fish after landing it. It was used to "give the last rites," thereby calling it a "Priest." The club shown is turned from hardwood. A hole is drilled in the end and filled with lead, then a wooden plug driven in place. A hole in the opposite end is used to thread a leather wrist thong through.

An old fisherman's tool was a "priest," a club used to deliver "the last rites." You can easily make one.

WOODEN PLUG

MELTED LEAD

1" SQUARES MADE FROM MAPLE, HICKORY OR ASH

LEATHER THONG

Jerky is an ideal way of utilizing the tougher cuts of game meat. One of the best ways of making jerky is with a jerky machine. The Jerky Master kit includes a gun and the seasonings.

Meat Preserving Tools

Ground game meat is extremely popular made into sausage. A wide range of sausage mixes, stuffers and other equipment is available from the Sausage Maker, L.E.M. and Bass Pro Shops.

Jerky is an ideal way to utilize the tougher cuts of game meat. You can make jerky in the traditional method by slicing the meat into thin strips, or these days you can utilize a jerky machine that extrudes ground meat into thin strips or rounds. The Jerky Master kit, from Hi Mountain Seasonings, comes complete with the Jerky Master Gun built specifically for making jerky out of ground meat. It's a high-impact machine that's extremely easy to use and clean. Two forming heads are included for making either strips or rounds. Also included is an industrial-grade jerky screen that fits ovens, barbeques and most smokers. This prevents jerky from falling between oven racks. Two jerky seasoning kits are included that make as little as one pound at a time or up to 15 pounds.

Although jerky can be dried in an oven, a dehydrator can make the chore easier. We've used an Excalibur dehydrator for many years. We've also used the Bradley smoker for drying and curing jerky and sausage.

In the past we double wrapped meat in plastic wrap, followed by butcher paper. Once we acquired a vacuum packing machine we now simply vacuum pack all meat.

The meat is ground, spices added and the mixture extruded through the jerky gun.

The extruded jerky is then dried in a dehydrator.

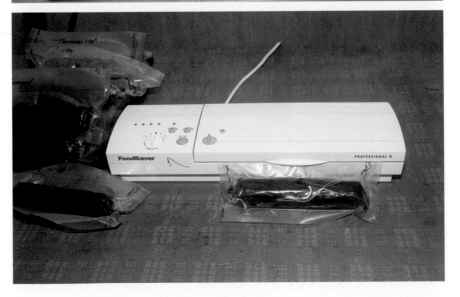

The best method of preserving meat by freezing is to first vacuum pack it in a machine such as the Professional II FoodSaver fromTilia. This removes oxygen and greatly extends storage time.

This is actually the ultimate method of preserving by freezing. The vacuum packing machine, such as the Professional II FoodSaver from Tilia, removes oxygen from the container and greatly extends storage time in the freezer and with less chance for freezer burn. Oxidation (exposure to the air) is the main cause of food spoilage. When foods absorb oxygen, they begin a process of irreversible chemical change. Contact with oxygen causes foods to lose nutrition and value, texture, flavor and overall quality.

When oxygen is removed from the storage environment, foods can be stored three to fives time longer than with conventional storage methods. In the absence of oxygen, dried, frozen and perishable foods requiring refrigeration will retain their freshness and flavor much longer, resulting in less food waste.

Oxygen enables microorganisms such as bacteria, mold and yeast to grow. These microorganisms cause rapid deterioration of food. Exposure to freezing-cold air also causes freezer burn in frozen foods. (Freezer burn is localized dehydration.) Oxygen causes foods that are moderately high in fats and oils to yield a rancid flavor. Air carries moisture and moisture causes the food to become soggy and lose its texture. Moisture causes caking of dry solids, making them difficult to handle. Oxygen also allows insects to survive and hatch.

The FoodSaver uses a powerful piston pump to create a vacuum of commercial quality. The FoodSaver is a sophisticated piece of equipment, yet very simple to operate. With a bag in place, the FoodSaver vacuums and seals with just one touch. Game meat and fish can be packaged whole, or as fillets that are prepared in meal-sized portions. Once it's put inside the bag, a vacuum is pulled and the bag is sealed, with all the air, odors and foreign tastes left on the outside. The compact, finished package can be easily weighed and marked with the date, description and weight, all with no mess.

Patented, 3-ply, FDA-approved FoodSaver bags and rolls are made of plastic with a nylon outer layer. They are strong and will not leak, so the vacuum is intact and the food stays fresh for months or even years in the freezer. The bags can be boiled, microwaved, cleaned (even in a dishwasher) and reused. Bags can also be custom-made to fit the size of the meat cut or fish. Foods that need to be refrigerated or frozen still need refrigeration or freezing even when vacuum packed.

Several FoodSaver models are available. The FoodSaver Professional II, Tilia's most advanced model, is ideal for packing fresh fish, seafood and meats. The unit has a special feature that makes a tight seal even when there is excess liquid. Plus, you can vacuum pack 50 bags at a time without having to let the machine's sealing element cool down, especially important when packaging the meat from a big game animal.

Smokers

Smoke cooking with indirect heat, or hot smoking (barbequing) with direct heat are both excellent methods for cooking game meats. In both methods the moisture is kept in the meat, producing a very tasty, tender meat without the dryness or grease that is

Many game meats are excellent hot smoked or barbequed.

Electric smokers, such as the Luhr-Jensen Little Chief, can be used to cold smoke sausages, fish and other game meats.

often connected with other types of cooking such as frying. Three types of smokers are available. The first is a simple barbeque grill, either charcoal or gas. Charcoal adds to the flavor, and wood chips can be added to a gas grill for added flavor, although they tend to flare up.

Grilled, bacon-wrapped doves are a favorite with our family. Marinate doves in a teriyaki sauce in the refrigerator for a couple of hours, and then wrap each dove breast in a piece of bacon held in place with toothpicks. Grill over hot coals for about five to eight minutes. Discard the bacon and serve.

We use the same tactic to create some of the most tender, tasty venison or elk filet mignons you can wrap your teeth around. The loins are cut at least an inch thick; meat tenderizer is used just as for any steak, unseasoned on one side and seasoned on the opposite. Once tenderized, the steaks are marinated in teriyaki sauce for a couple of hours. They are then removed from the marinade and bacon is wrapped around them, held in place with toothpicks. Grill over hot coals approximately six to eight minutes per side or to suit.

The second type of smoker is the electric smoker. Some of these also have an enclosure to hold the meat, a heat and smoke source and a pan to hold liquids, water or a marinade. We've tested two, the economical, but very efficient Luhr-Jenson and the Bradley Smoker. Both do an excellent job and make the chore easy and simple. You can also make you own electric smoker from an old refrigerator or even a large wooden box. Luhr-Jensen also sells a complete line of cures, brines and flavorings, as well as their Chips 'n Chunks wood chips. The Little Chief is an excellent fish smoker. To use, brine the fish overnight. Then load the smoker with fish, plug in the smoker and smoke thick chunks for eight to twelve hours, using three pans of Chips 'n Chunks in the fuel pan. The Bradley Smoker has a thermometer, and the heat can be regulated by moving a switch.

One unit I tested extensively in writing my Field Dressing and Butchering book series is the Bradley Smoker. This unusual electric smoker features an automatic smoke generator, with a separate heating element that has infinite control up to 320°F. An insulated cabinet makes it extremely efficient and eliminates drastic temperature fluctuations. It smokes with self-loading Flavor Bisquettes producing smoke for up to eight hours, and then shuts off automatically. A liquid pan is placed in the bottom for water or marinades. I've found the moist smokers to be fantastic for producing great jerky when used without the marinade pan, as well as for smoking fish such as trout or salmon with the marinade pan.

Bass Pro Shops also carry their SmokinTex, a very large electric smoker that will hold up to 33 pounds of meat and has a dual heating element and an optional deflector plate that directs the drippings onto or away from the wood boxes to reduce the amount of moisture in the smoker. They also carry the Masterbilt Electric Smoker which has a thermostat controlled heating element and four trays.

The SmokeVault, from Camp Chef, has a 25,000-BTU propane burner, a stainless steel water pan and a cast-iron wood chip box. It also features an easy push-button igniter and four removable, adjustable smoking racks.

True smokers, however, use indirect heat and are quite often larger models of welded metal to maintain more consistent heat, and are capable of handling much more fire as well as more meat at one loading. True smokers cook by indirect heat, with the coals in one area of the smoker and the meat in another. A number of these smokers are available, but the best I've tested is the Good-One Grill and Smoker from Ron Goodwin Enterprises. The Good-One is available in several sizes from small to large commercial models. All are built with the same basic design. The front lower compartment is the firebox and grill. You can grill just as you would with any charcoal grill. The

The Bradley Smoker has an automatic smoke generator with a separate heating element that has infinite control up to 320° F.

The Good-One Smoker is a true indirect heat smoker that will smoke larger meat cuts such as wild turkey, ribs, deer loins and hams.

upper back compartment, however, is for smoking or cooking meats with lower, indirect heat. On the lower front of the firebox are the air control dampers to control the heat in the firebox and grill area. On the top of the smoker lid is an exhaust vent. The heat in the smoker is controlled by the dampers. The smokers are constructed with a clean-out pan located under the firebox grate.

To smoke, the top grate is removed from the bottom compartment and charcoal placed on the bottom grate. You'll need about 10 pounds of charcoal for several hours of smoking. After coals are burning, add the wood chunks to provide the smoke flavor and close the bottom lid. Just as in any smoking, the type of wood chunks used provides the flavoring. These types of smokers do not use water pans. "Water pans make steam heat, which can cause smoke to disappear rapidly and tends to make meat soggy," said Ron Goodwin. "We don't recommend water pans for true, old-fashioned pit barbecue flavor." Ron also suggests using pure charcoal chunks rather than briquettes, although the former are a little harder to obtain. "Another secret to good barbecue smoked meat is a smoker that will hold an even temperature and the right amount and kind of wood," Ron added. "Hickory, mesquite, oak, pecan, alder, fruit woods: cherry, peach, apple or grape vine are recommended. Poultry requires much less wood than other meats, and game birds and waterfowl are very good if smoked using fruit woods. The best result for smoke flavor is to use chunks of wood; two or three chunks, about three to four inches in size usually give a nice smoked flavor."

Maintaining an even temperature over a long period of time is important for ease in smoke cooking. The Good-One smoker has a temperature gauge and a variety of means of regulating the heat. By simply opening and closing the dampers you can control the heat precisely. You will also need a meat thermometer to check the internal temperature of your meat.

Smoke cooking is an excellent method for cooking venison roasts or hams (hind quarters) because it keeps the moisture in the meat rather than drying it out. Even the relatively dry meat of some of the big game and venison comes out moist and for the most part tender.

For a venison roast, ham or hind quarter cook at 275–300°F for two hours, then cut the smoker temperature back with the damper to 225°F. Finish cooking at that temperature for one hour for each pound of meat. Use a meat thermometer and cook until the internal temperature reaches 180–190°F. Wrapping venison in bacon strips will add some flavoring and also keep the meat from drying out.

I've also discovered that, regardless of the meat being smoked, I prefer to smoke for about an hour or two, and then wrap the meat in foil for the remainder of the cooking process. This tends to hold in even more moisture. The roast or ham can be basted with barbecue sauce or a number of other sauces or left natural.

TANNING AND TRAPPING

The ultimate to many outdoorsmen or women is tanning the game they take, or making decorative or useful items from the horns, feathers, bones and other parts of the animal. This is utilizing the most of the animal. Like the other outdoor pursuits, a good workplace is necessary. Much of the work of tanning and preparing traps and hides can be done outside in good weather, but a workplace out of the weather is best. The fur shed doesn't have to be fancy, and in fact most aren't, often a simple lean-to shed next to another building. A small lockable outbuilding is the best choice to store tools, materials and hides. Tanning and fur work isn't necessarily "smelly" to those who love it, but does have its own unique "odor." And, it can get messy, so a place at least a short distance from the house can keep peace in the family.

You'll need a sturdy table separate from the meat table for these chores, but it should still be easily cleaned. And, in many instances these chores are done outside, so it should be constructed of moisture-resistant woods. The table can be easily constructed of treated 2 x 4s with a solid treated plywood top, but it should be at least 36" high or a good working height.

One of the most important tools is a freezer to store hides and skins. It doesn't have to be large, but beats storing hides in with your frozen food. Of course you will need lots of skinning knives, large and small, and a fleshing knife. Gambrels and a pole to suspend the critter from for skinning are also necessary. Large plastic tubs are the best for holding chemicals when soaking hides.

With just a little time and materials you can easily create your own tanning and fur preparation tools. They can make working on big game and predator hides and furs easier and more productive.

Fleshing Board, Beam, and Breaking Stakes

One of the most important steps in tanning skins or hides, or for preparing furs for sale, is removing the flesh and membrane from the flesh side. A fleshing beam is necessary for this chore. Three types can be constructed: an outside beam, an inside heavy-duty beam for deer skins and other big game and a small workbench mounted beam for small furs, or even for working deer skins. I have all three and use them at different times of the year and for different purposes.

The first is an old-fashioned log beam placed outside. Fleshing and especially dehairing of hides can be messy, and this keeps the mess outside, weather permitting. The beam should be sized to the most common usage. A large beam, approximately 2" in diameter and about 8' long, is best for a large deer, moose or elk hide. A beam of 10–12" and about 6' long, however, will suffice and is a good size for a deer skin. I made

For tanning game hides
you'll need a fleshing beam.
This can be a large log set at
an angle outside.

Or you can make a smaller fleshing beam for inside use, clamping it to a workbench.

my outside beam quite simply from a section of sycamore tree. The wood choice is because sycamore doesn't have thick bark and it can easily be smoothed up with just a bit of work with a draw knife. The high end of the beam should be at a comfortable working height. I like mine just under my chest. The high end is held up in place with treated 2 x 4s while a 2 x 4 stake at the back end keeps it from shifting backwards.

You can also do a lot of tanning or fur preparation chores inside. Time spent in the fur shed during cold winter days can be enjoyable and profitable, and for this a stand-up beam can be constructed. This also allows you to work at a comfortable height. The framework is constructed of 2 x 4s while the beam is carved from a 2 x 6.

A smaller fleshing beam that can be attached to a workbench with a clamp or screws that allow it to be easily removed when not needed is also very useful. The beam can even be fastened to a wall and hinged to swing up out of the way when not in use. Both the larger and smaller fleshing beam ends can be shaped with a saber or band saw and a draw knife, or better yet, a portable electric belt sander. The ends of the beams must be rounded and with a front top edge sloping down to a fairly sharp edge. This allows you to hold the hide in place on the beam with your belly while working the fleshing knife with both hands.

You will also need a fleshing knife and buckets or barrels to receive the scrapings.

Of course, the simplest method is with an old-fashioned Arkansas stone and lots of patience.

Famed knifemaker Kershaw has a pair of pocket-sized sharpeners, the Edge-Tek and Ultra-Tek. Both feature rods that screw into a metal tube for easy carrying in your pocket or pack. The Edge-Tek is for straight blades and the Ultra-Tek is tapered for use with serrated blades. A belt-loop carrying case keeps the Edge-Tek handy for instant use.

Kershaw's Arkansas Stone Sharpener, also sold as Smith's GetSharp Knife Sharpening System, is a two-stage system that is easily hand held and small enough to pack. It comes with carbide cutting heads for the initial sharpening. A natural Arkansas stone is then used for final honing. Holes are provided for screws so the unit can be permanently mounted on a workbench or any flat surface.

Gatco's Tri-Seps Triangular Hone Serration, Edge Point Sharpening System was designed in collaboration with the Army Airforce Exchange Service for use by troops in the field. Extremely lightweight, compact and versatile, it is an alumina ceramic hone with a lifetime guarantee against wearing out. The Tri-Seps is $3^1/_2$" long with triangular construction. There's a deep groove for pointed instruments and hook sharpening as well as PVC slip-resistant end caps with lanyard hole and angle guide. It comes with a 6" beaded key chain.

The Hughes Products HPX2 knife sharpener has two sets of honing rods, tungsten carbide for initial sharpening and ceramic for final work, in one simple, field-ready unit. Both have the blades angled precisely to shape the cutting edges on camp knives.

Lansky is the home of Crock Stick Sharpeners, and their new Multi-Sharpener features a unique triangular Crock Stick. The three flat surfaces on the stick can be used for sharpening straight-edge knives or tools including knives, axe heads, shovels and machetes. The triangular corner edges are made for sharpening serrated, scalloped or saw-tooth blades. A special groove on one side is for sharpening fish hooks and other pointed objects. The Multi-Sharpener is extremely compact and lightweight. It also comes with a handy key chain.

The EZE-Lap Diamond Sharpeners are steel sharpening rods and come in several sizes and shapes from pocket to larger kitchen-style steels. Diamond particles are permanently attached to a strong metal backing surface with a patented process.

The Flipstik from Hewlett Manufacturing is a very compact, lightweight, three-sided diamond sharpener that fits in your pocket. A rod attachment makes the Flipstik adaptable to any clamp-guide system.

Innovative Products Handy Sharp hones and sharpens knives and fish hooks. It is also lightweight and compact enough to fit in your pocket, tacklebox or fanny pack. The Handy Sharp has tungsten carbide cutting and honing edges for quick and easy dual honing. Katz Knives produces some of the best knives on the market, and they also carry a full line of Genuine Arkansas Whetstones for those who prefer to do their sharpening in the old-fashioned but extremely effective method. These stones are well known for their ability to sharpen and polish blades without removing excessive amounts of metal. Honing oil is supplied with many of the Katz sharpeners.

MAKING KNIVES

If you purchase ready-made blades the tools you'll need are those for installing handles. And the type of handles you install dictates the amount of tools needed. Many blades are full tang or feature a flat tang running the width of the handle pieces. These are commonly held in place with rivets or pins. Handles are often bone, stag or antler or wood. A drill press and drill bits are needed for boring the holes in the handle materials. A means of riveting or driving pins is also needed. A large vise, small anvil and a small ball-peen hammer are commonly used. The handle and blades are then ground together to create a unified shape. The best tool for this purpose is a belt grinder. These typically feature a 1" or 2" wide belt with a flexible head, and a table with a belt stop. These may also be called belt sanders. Many of these are combined with a grinding wheel on the side. Or they may feature a disc sander on the side. Grizzly offers several of these tools including their Knife Belt Sander/Buffer. It features a 2" belt with a quick-change mechanism that allows the belt to be changed in seconds. An auxiliary arbor accepts buffing wheels, sanding drums and flap sanders. The belt arm can also be fully tilted. Some knife tangs are very narrow. These are normally glued in a hole bored in the handle material, such as an antler base or stag handle. You'll need a drill press, and a means of holding the handle secure. A drill-press vise is the best tool, but a large wood clamp can also be used.

I've made a number of knife blades, grinding them from recycled metal pieces. An old file is a popular choice as is a piece of automobile spring. Heavy-duty sawmill

Making knives is a lot of fun. You'll need a drill press, drill bits, a riveting set or pins for driving handle pins and rivets in place.

Belt grinders can be used to shape and grind knife blades.

band saw blades make excellent fillet knives, as does an old heavy-duty handsaw. Again, you'll need a sturdy grinder, preferably a two-wheel grinder. And you'll need a means of honing and sharpening, as well as installing handles. You will also need a propane torch and metal water container for "quenching" the newly ground blade.

The biggest step is when you begin forging your own blades. My son Michael is a well-known custom knife maker and not only grinds modern-day metals into beautiful custom knives, but also occasionally hand-hammers his own Damascus blades. When you get into forging, you'll need a forge, an anvil, tongs, hammers, a well-ventilated area to work and a fire extinguisher.

A propane torch and means of quenching metal is necessary for knife work as well.

Making leather sheaths requires leatherworking tools.

Sheath Making

Most sheaths are made of leather, but these days modern materials such as Kydex are used to "mold" around a knife blade for a unique appearance and a rugged, long-lasting sheath with a modern design. For leather work you'll need a sharp utility or Xacto knife with a variety of blades. You will need a leather punch, an awl, lacing needle or hand-held automatic stitching machine and a solid wood surface to work on. You may also wish to do some leather embellishment with stamping and carving.

L.E.M. Products, Inc., 877-536-7763, www.lemproducts.com

Lindy Little Joe, 218-829-1714, www.lindyfishingtackle.com

Luhr-Jensen & Sons, Inc., 800-366-3811, www.luhrjensen.com

Magic Products, 715-824-3100, www.magicproducts.com

Marine Metal Products Co., Inc., 727-461-5575, www.marinemetal.com

McGowan Manufacturing, 320-587-2222

Meyerco Manufacturing, 214-467-8949

Miles Gilbert, *see* Battenfeld Technologies

Mister Twister, Mepps, 800-637-7703, www.mepps.com

Plano Molding, 800-874-6905, www.planomolding.com

Rapala, 952-933-7060, www.rapala.com

Rockler, 800-233-9359, www.rocklerpro.com

The Sausage Maker, Inc., 888-490-8525, www.sausagemaker.com

Shooters Choice Gun Care, 800-232-1991, www.shooters-choice.com

Smith Abrasives, Inc., 501-321-2244, www.getsharp.com

Suntuf, Inc., 800-999-9459, www.suntuf.com

Tempress Products, www.tempressproducts.com

Tipton Gun Vise, *see* Battenfeld Technologies

Tru Hone, 800-237-4663, www.truhone.com

VillaWare, 800-248-9687, www.villaware.com

Wheeler Engineering, *see* Battenfeld Technologies

Index